Mini Knitted
CHRISTMAS

Dedication

This book is dedicated to Daddy Father Christmas x

Mini Knitted
CHRISTMAS

Sue Stratford

Search Press

First published in 2015

Search Press Limited
Wellwood, North Farm Road,
Tunbridge Wells, Kent TN2 3DR

Suppliers
If you have difficulty in obtaining any of the materials and
equipment mentioned in this book, then please visit the
Search Press website for details of suppliers:
www.searchpress.com

You are invited to view the author's work at:
www.suestratford.co.uk
www.theknittinghut.co.uk
Knittinghutsue on Ravelry
Sue Stratford Knits on Facebook
Knittinghutsue on Instagram
Knittinghutsue on Twitter

Printed in China

Acknowledgements
This book would not have happened without Heather
and our four-hour journey home from The Knitting
& Stitching Show thinking up all these Christmas
projects. Thanks also go to the very long-suffering,
marvellous May Corfield and Jacky Edwards for
making sense where there was none.
Thank you to the fantastic test knitters –
Susan Edwards, Janet Davison, Bekky Bush and
Mandy Wendes – together with everyone else at
Team Hut for their advice and positive comments.
Thanks must also go to Bill Horn for his advice, as a
structural engineer, on the construction of the stable.
Thank you also to my lovely family – Christmas has
overrun a bit this year!

Contents

Mary and Joseph

Baby Jesus

Angel Gabriel

Three Kings

Shepherd and Sheep

Little Donkey

Shooting Star

Stable

Santa Claus

Sleigh

Reindeer

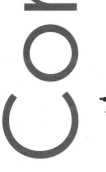

Christmas Projects 44

Mini Gifts

Mistletoe

Penguins

Gingerbread Folk

Candy Canes

Turkey

Christmas Crackers

Elf

Tree Baubles

Paper Chains

Polar Bears

Reindeer Heads

Christmas Lanterns

Holly Fairy

Magic Elf Boots

Introduction

This book came about because customers kept asking me at various knitting shows, 'When are you doing another Christmas book? I've knitted everything in the first one.' When I began to think about it, there were endless possibilities for a second book with even more projects.

I have had so much fun working out the projects in this book, from a full mini nativity to Santa in his sleigh, together with his nine reindeer (yes, I had to make all nine!). It also includes mistletoe, cute and cuddly penguins and polar bears. I think this book has Christmas wrapped up.

Some of the projects, such as the mini gifts, look beautiful in Santa's sleigh, and would look equally delightful strung together with invisible thread and hung on a Christmas tree. Rudolph and friends would also look great galloping through the branches.

All the projects use small amounts of yarn, and all the yarns are repeated throughout the book – so if you buy a few balls of yarn you will be able to use them for multiple projects.

As the projects are so tiny, I haven't stated the exact amount of yarn I have used as, in the majority of cases, it is under 10g per project. The larger projects, such as the stable and sleigh, do show yarn amounts, as this is essential.

The tension for the projects is not shown either. This is because you will be knitting the yarn on much smaller knitting needles than you would usually use. All but one of the projects (the turkey) are knitted using 4-ply (fingering) yarn, which has a recommended needle size of 3.25mm (UK 10, US 3). In this book, however, you will be using 2.75mm (UK 12, US 2) needles to create a tighter finish – this will give a better shape and definition to your finished projects, and ensure that the toy

stuffing does not show through. As a rough guide, you should be getting between 7 and 9 stitches per 2.5cm (1in).

Sewing together your finished work is what gives the projects character, and you will find very informative sections showing you how to complete the heads for all the nativity figures and sew the reindeer and donkey together. In addition, there are detailed step-by-step tutorials for some of the techniques used, such as how to make an i-cord and three-needle cast-off, together with some for the more decorative stitches used, such as chain stitch.

I hope that this book will inspire you to create your own Mini Knitted Christmas!

Materials and tools

Yarn

All the yarns used in this book are repeated throughout. You will notice that the mini gifts, Christmas lanterns and paper chains all use the same colours. These colours are also used for the three kings. If you buy a selection of colours, you can make a range of projects from the book, as each one uses only a small quantity.

All the yarns used (except for the turkey, which uses a double knitting yarn) are 4-ply (fingering) weight. This is to give the definition and detail that small projects require. If you would prefer larger results, then just substitute the yarn for double knitting yarn and use 3mm (UK 11, US 2/3) knitting needles. The projects will work just as well, but they will come out slightly larger.

I have used alpaca and merino yarns, as I love the feel of them and the beautiful saturated colours, but you can use whichever yarn you fancy in whatever colours you like – let your imagination run wild!

I have also used some metallic gold and silver yarn for details, and some sparkly white baby yarn that looks great as a penguin's tummy. The 2-ply (laceweight) yarn I have used is a mohair mix and is often worked using a double strand, which makes it equivalent to a 4-ply (fingering) yarn.

Needles

I have used 2.75mm (UK 12, US 2) knitting needles for most of the projects, which ensures that your work is tight enough for the toy stuffing not to show through and for the finished project to hold its shape. As the pieces are so small, I prefer to work on double-pointed knitting needles, not for any other reason than they are short and I find them easier to work with.

I love using wooden needles, as they are particularly smooth and light to work with, but I know that every knitter has their own preference when it comes to needles – so use whichever needles you love, and these projects will knit up really quickly!

Other materials

To give the projects that finishing touch, I have used a variety of different materials. All the materials used in this book are easily obtained from a craft supplier, or you may find you already have some of them in your stash!

The beads I have used for the eyes of the animals and figures give them a real twinkle, but you could use embroidery silks and embroider the eyes instead, especially if you are planning to give the finished item to a small child.

The chenille sticks are great to give structure to a project, such as the reindeer, and allow you to bend the legs to add character. The gold loops used for the reindeer are jump rings, used in jewellery making, and Rudolph is also finished off with a small brass bell.

For embroidering features on the small figures, I used sewing cotton. I also used sewing cotton and a sewing needle to sew the smaller beads in place. Try to match the colour of the sewing cotton to the yarn colour you are sewing into, in order to disguise it.

Useful stitches

Kitchener stitch

Also known as grafting, Kitchener stitch allows you to join two sets of stitches that are still on the needle (or 'live') by using a tapestry needle threaded with yarn to create a row that looks like knitted stitches between them.

1 Taking your needle and 'tail' of yarn, divide the stitches evenly between the two needles and hold the needles with the points in the same direction and the WS together. The working yarn should be at the back.
2 Insert your tapestry needle into the first stitch on the front needle, purlwise, and pull the yarn through, leaving the stitch on the needle.
3 Insert the needle into the first stitch on the back needle, knitwise, and pull the yarn through, leaving the stitch on the needle.

These two stitches are the 'set up' stitches. The following instructions will be repeated until all your stitches are worked:

4 Insert the needle into the first stitch on the front needle knitwise and slip it off the needle.
5 Insert the needle into the next stitch on the front needle purlwise and pull the yarn through, leaving the stitch on the needle.
6 Insert the needle into the first stitch on the back needle purlwise and slip it off the needle.
7 Insert the needle into the next stitch on the back needle knitwise and pull the yarn through, leaving the stitch on the needle.
8 Repeat steps 4–7, tightening the stitches as you go.

Blanket stitch

This stitch is used to outline the gingerbread girl's dress on page 66 (see also right).

1 Thread a needle with yarn and bring to the front of your work about 1cm (3/8in) from the edge.
2 Leaving a small gap along the edge of the work, take the needle to the back of the work approximately 1cm (3/8in) in from the edge and bring it back to the front at the edge of the knitting.
3 Loop your yarn under the needle and pull it through until it lies neatly against the emerging yarn.
4 Repeat this process to create more stitches. Use the photograph opposite for guidance.

Wrap and turn

This technique ensures you do not end up with a 'hole' in your knitting when working short row shaping and turning your work mid-row.

1 Work to the point where you need to wrap and turn (w&t).
2 Move the yarn to the other side of your work, taking it between the needles.
3 Slip the following stitch from your left needle to the right needle.
4 Bring the yarn around the stitch and back through the needles.
5 Slip the stitch back to your left hand needle
6 Turn the work and continue.
7 When you reach the wrapped stitch, slip it onto your right-hand needle and, using the point of your left-hand needle, pick up the wrap of yarn, slip the stitch and wrap back to your left-hand needle, then work the stitch and wrap together. This will make the turn in your work less noticeable.

Hints & Tips ✳ ✳ ✳ ✳ ✳ ✳

Leave a length of yarn on your knitted pieces so that you can use it to sew the section together. This will save you having to darn a short end in and attach a new length of yarn.

I always try out the positioning of eyes before sewing them in place by using small glass-headed pins, which you can push in where you think the eyes should be before you make your final decision.

You can hide the ends of yarn inside your projects when you sew them together and stuff them. That way, you have fewer ends to darn in!

Abbreviations

cm	centimetre(s)
DK	double knitting yarn
GS	garter stitch (knit every row)
in	inch(es)
K	knit
Kfb	knit into the front and back of the stitch, making one more stitch
Kfbf	knit into the front, back and front of the stitch, making two more stitches
K2tog	knit two stitches together
mm	millimetre(s)
M1	make a backwards loop on your needle by twisting the yarn towards you and slipping the resulting loop onto the right-hand needle. On the following row, knit or purl through the back of the stitch. This produces a very neat result.
P	purl
Pfb	purl into the front and back of the stitch, making one more stitch
psso	pass slipped stitch over
P1B	P1B: purl the next stitch together with corresponding loop from cast-on edge
P2tog	purl two stitches together
P2togtbl	purl two stitches together, through the back of the loops
rem	remaining
RS	right side of work
sl1	slip one st from left-hand needle to right-hand needle without working it
SS	stocking stitch (knit one row, purl one row)
ssK	slip 2 sts knitwise one at a time, pass the two slipped stitches back to the left needle, knit both together through the back of the loop
st(s)	stitch(es)
tog	together
w&t	wrap and turn (see opposite)
YO	yarn over

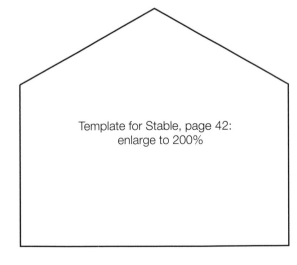

Template for Stable, page 42:
enlarge to 200%

Sewing up the reindeer

These instructions can be used for sewing up both the reindeer and the little donkey.

1 Starting at the cast-on edge (nose) and using dark brown hand-dyed yarn, run a line of stitches along the cast-on edge, gather and secure. Continue by sewing the seam along the lower edge of the reindeer. Continue sewing the seam under the reindeer's belly, filling with toy stuffing as you go. Then fill the head and neck section with toy stuffing, leaving the seam at the neck open so that it looks like the photograph above.

2 Taking a needle threaded with yarn, join the yarn at the base of the neck. Fold the neck upwards so the reindeer's head is upright (see photographs for guidance) and sew the cast-off edge at the base of the neck to the body section, 3 rows towards the back of the reindeer from the cast-on edge. This ensures that the head is upright.

3 Starting with the front legs, measure the chenille stick against a knitted leg, fold in half where the bottom of the leg will be and thread the chenille stick through. (The chenille stick is easier to thread through when folded double.) Trim near to the body so that the second leg section is a double length of chenille stick.

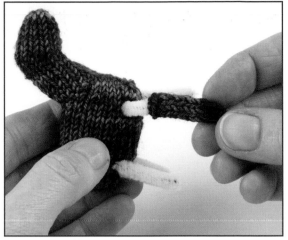

4 Repeat this process for the back legs.

5 Using dark brown yarn, run a line of stitches along the cast-on edge of the leg, gather and secure. Sew the rest of the 'foot' using dark brown yarn. Change to hand-dyed yarn and sew the remainder of the seam up the leg. Leave the cast-off edge open. Slide the leg up the chenille stick, ensuring that the seam is on the inside edge.

6 Carefully sew the top of the leg to the body. Repeat for the other three legs.

The reindeer, sewn up and stuffed. For the rest of the reindeer's features, please see pages 56–57.

Making the heads

These detailed instructions will make it much easier to create the features on the nativity figures, the holly fairy, the elf and Santa Claus.

Before starting, sew the head together as follows. Using matching yarn, gather the cast-off edge of the head and secure. Sew the side seam, which goes at the back of the head. Fill with toy stuffing as you go. When you reach the cast-on edge, run a line of stitches along it, then gather and secure.

1 Taking a sewing needle threaded with matching sewing cotton, attach it to the base of the head and thread upwards through the head to emerge at the top right-hand side of the nose.

2 Thread a bead onto the needle and sew back into the head to emerge at the base.

3 Pull the sewing cotton so that the eye is pulled back into the head slightly. Secure at the base. This gives the appearance of 'cheeks' and a more realistic finish.

4 Repeat for the second eye, leaving approximately one and a half stitches between each eye.

5 Thread your needle with black sewing cotton and secure at the base of the head. Bring the needle up through the head as shown, to the left-hand side just under the nose.

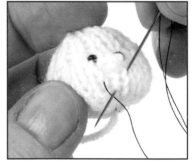

6 Leaving a gap of approximately two stitches, thread your needle back into the head and bring the needle out one stitch lower, in the centre of the two stitches.

7 Making sure that the working thread is above the loop, pull the needle through and downwards to make the 'smile'.

8 Thread the needle back to the base and secure, being careful not to pull too tightly and distort the shape of the mouth.

9 Taking a cotton bud, pick up some pink blusher, and blot on a tissue.

10 Carefully dab two spots on the cheeks. You can build up the colour gradually by adding more blusher.

11 To make the hair, thread a darning needle with a strand of yellow yarn. Secure the yarn at the back of the head. This will not show when you have completed the head.

12 Threading your needle into the head along the hair line, make a straight stitch by pulling the needle and yarn back through the head.

13 Repeat this process to create a line of stitches right around the hairline. This will then give you a guide and you can make more stitches to fill in between them and create the hair.
Note: The nativity figures with straight hair have headdresses to cover the back of the head.

A completed head for one of the nativity figures.

Decorative stitches

These stitches are used throughout the book to decorate many of the projects.

Chain stitch

1 Start by bringing your threaded needle from the back of the knitting to the front.

2 Re-insert the needle from the front to the back into the same stitch you came out of, forming a loop. Bring the needle point back through to the front of the knitting, approximately one stitch from where it went in, so that the needle comes through the inside of the loop of yarn.

3 Pull the needle through the knitting to form the first chain.

4 Repeat steps 2 and 3 to create more stitches. When you have as many stitches as you need, thread the needle to the back of the knitting, looping the yarn over the final stitch, and securing it on the wrong side.

5 Your finished line of stitches can be straight or wavy, as required.

Chain stitch details on a mini gift (see page 58).

Whipped running stitch

1 Securing the yarn at the back of the knitting, bring the needle through to the front of the work. Thread the needle through the knitting to the back of the work, approximately one stitch apart. Repeat this process to make a line of stitches.

2 When you get to the end of your line, thread the needle to the front of the work in the centre of the first stitch.

3 Thread the needle and yarn underneath the second stitch as shown.

4 Repeat along the line of stitches to make a 'solid' line of stitches. Take the needle and yarn to the back of the knitting and secure.

Whipped running stitch is used on the king's gown (see page 32).

French knot

1 Secure the yarn on the reverse side and bring the sewing needle and yarn through to the front of the work, then thread the needle through a stitch, as shown.

2 Wind the yarn around the needle twice.

3 Pull the needle upwards through the knitting, holding the loops around the needle with your fingers while pulling the yarn.

4 Thread the needle and yarn back through to the reverse of the knitting. The loops of yarn you made will now form a knot. Fasten off the yarn securely.

French knots make up Angel Gabriel's hair (see page 30).

Other techniques

How to make an i-cord

The i-cord technique is a really quick and easy way to make a knitted cord that gives the appearance of French knitting. You will need double-pointed knitting needles. I have used this technique for the sleigh's runners, the top loop of the lantern, the candy canes, mistletoe sprigs and the holly fairy's arms. If you do not want to use this technique, just knit the piece flat, using stocking stitch, and carefully sew the side seam.

The sleigh, complete with i-cord runners (see page 50).

1 Cast on the required number of stitches using double-pointed knitting needles.

2 Knit all the stitches.

3 Slide the stitches to the opposite end of the needle, pulling the yarn behind the stitches.

4 Pulling the yarn around the back of the stitches, knit the stitches again.

5 Repeat steps 3 and 4. By pulling the yarn behind the stitches on the needle, you close the 'gap' and give the fabric the appearance of French knitting.

6 To finish off, cut the yarn and, using a darning needle, thread the yarn through the stitches, tighten and fasten off.

A Christmas lantern with an i-cord hanging loop (see page 88).

Three-needle cast-off

This technique gives a really neat result and also saves sewing up a seam. I have used it for the nativity figures' headdresses, the reindeer and the elf boots, among others.

1 Divide the remaining stitches evenly between two needles and place with right sides together.

2 Taking a third needle, knit the first stitch from each needle together.

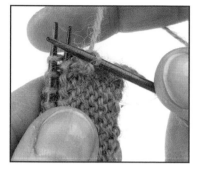

3 You now have one stitch on your right-hand needle.

4 Knit the next stitch from each needle together, so you have two stitches on the right-hand needle.

5 Cast off the first stitch in the usual way, by lifting it over the second stitch.

6 You now have one stitch on the right-hand needle. Repeat steps 4 and 5 until you have one stitch remaining on your right-hand needle. Thread the yarn through the stitch to secure, and fasten off.

The reindeer's bottom has a seam worked in three-needle cast-off (see page 54).

7 This shows the wrong side of the work with a really neat cast-off seam.

8 This shows the right side of the work.

Nativity Projects

Mary and Joseph

Instructions

Note: For the wrap and turn (w&t) technique, see page 12.

Head: make two

Using cream yarn, cast on 13 sts and purl 1 row.

Next row: K1, M1, (K2, M1) five times, K2 (19 sts).

Starting with a purl row, work 3 rows in SS.

Next row: K9, Kfb, turn (20 sts).

Next row: P2, turn.

Next row: Knit to end of row.

Next row: P9, P2tog, P9 (19 sts).

Next row: K5, (ssK) twice, K1, (K2tog) twice, K5 (15 sts).

Starting with a purl row, work 3 rows in SS.

Next row: K1, K2tog, K2, K2tog, K1, K2tog, K2, K2tog, K1 (11 sts).

Thread yarn through rem sts, leaving a length of yarn for sewing up.

Body: make two

Using cream yarn, cast on 8 sts and purl 1 row.

Next row: K2, M1, K4, M1, K2 (10 sts).

Next row: P2, M1, P1, M1, P4, M1, P1, M1, P2 (14 sts).

Next row: K3, M1, K1, M1, K6, M1, K1, M1, K3 (18 sts).

Starting with a purl row, work 11 rows in SS.

Next row (RS): Purl (this forms a fold line).

Next row: (P2tog nine times (9 sts).

Next row: Knit.

Thread yarn through rem sts, leaving a length of yarn for sewing up.

Gown: make one in blue yarn and one in fawn yarn

Using blue yarn for Mary or fawn yarn for Joseph, cast on 10 sts and purl 2 rows.

Next row: K2, M1, K1, M1, K4, M1, K1, M1, K2 (14 sts).

Next row: P3, M1, P1, M1, P6, M1, P1, M1, P3 (18 sts).

Next row: K4, M1, K1, M1, K8, M1, K1, M1, K4 (22 sts).

Starting with a purl row, work 3 rows in SS.

Next row: K2, (M1, K4) five times (27 sts).

Starting with a purl row, work 3 rows in SS.

Next row: (K4, M1) six times, K3 (33 sts).

Starting with a purl row, work 3 rows in SS.

Next row: K3, (K2tog, K3) six times (27 sts). Cast off.

Sleeves: make two in blue yarn and two in fawn yarn

Using blue yarn for Mary or fawn yarn for Joseph, cast on 7 sts and, starting with a knit row, work 2 rows in SS.

Materials

For Mary: 4-ply (fingering) yarn in cream, blue, sparkly white, metallic gold and yellow

For Joseph: 4-ply (fingering) yarn in cream, fawn, green and dark brown

Toy stuffing

Black sewing cotton and sewing needle

4 x black seed beads

Needles

2.75mm (UK 12, US 2)

Size

6.5cm (2½in) high

Next row: K1, M1, K to last st, M1, K1 (9 sts).

Purl 1 row.

Repeat last two rows twice more (13 sts). Cast off.

Hands: make four

Using cream yarn, cast on 3 sts and, starting with a knit row, work 8 rows in SS. Cast off.

Headddress

Using sparkly white yarn for Mary or fawn yarn for Joseph, cast on 26 sts and purl 2 rows.

Starting with a knit row, work 4 rows in SS.

Next row: K8, w&t.

Next row: Purl to end of row.

Knit 1 row.

Next row: P8, w&t.

Next row: Knit to end of row.

Next row: P7, (P2tog) six times, P7 (20 sts).

Divide rem sts evenly between two needles and join using Kitchener stitch (see page 12). Alternatively, use the three-needle cast-off technique (see page 21).

Mary's halo

Using metallic gold yarn, cast on 6 sts.
Next row: (Kfb) six times (12 sts).
Knit 1 row.
Next row: (Kfb), twelve times (24 sts).
Knit 2 rows.
Next row: (K1, Kfb) twelve times (36 sts).
Knit 1 row.
Cast off.

Joseph's scarf

Using green yarn, cast on 5 sts and work
in GS until work measures 7cm (2¾in).
Cast off.

Joseph's beard

Using dark brown yarn, cast on 2 sts and
knit 1 row.
Next row: K1, M1, K1 (3 sts).

Knit 1 row.
Next row: (K1, M1) twice, K1 (5 sts).
Continuing in GS, cast on 3 sts at the
beginning of the next 2 rows (11 sts).
Cast off.

Making up

Mary

Following the instructions on page 16, sew
the head together and add the features,
using yellow yarn to embroider the hair at
the front of the head (the headdress will
cover the back).

Starting at the gathered edge of the
body, sew along the seam, filling with toy
stuffing as you go. Run a line of stitches
around the cast-on stitches, gather
and fasten.

Sew the head to the body, ensuring the
seams are towards the back. Lightly press

the gown and place on Mary. Sew the long
seam, which will be at the back.

Fold each hand in half and sew the
seam around the hand.

Take a sleeve and a hand. Sew the hand
to the inside edge of the cast-off edge of
the sleeve, using the sleeve yarn so that
the stitches do not show on the outside.

Repeat for the second hand and sleeve.

Note: Sew one hand to the left of the
cast-off edge and the other to the right.
When sewing the sleeves to the body
make sure the side the hand is sewn to
is against the body.

Once the hand has been sewn in place,
sew the side seam of the sleeve, placing it
underneath when you sew it to the body.

Pin each sleeve in place towards the
back of the body, using the photograph for
guidance. Sew the sleeves in place.

Lightly press the headdress and pin in
place onto the head. Sew in place.

Run a gathering thread through the
cast-on edge of the halo, tighten and sew
the side seam. Pin the halo on the back of
Mary's head and then sew in place (see
photograph on page 24).

Joseph

Following the instructions on page 16,
sew the head together and add the eyes
and hair, using dark brown yarn for the
hair. Using dark brown yarn, embroider a
moustache, using straight stitches, and
sew the beard in place, leaving a gap for
the mouth.

Sew the body, gown, sleeves and hands
as for Mary. Lightly press the headdress
and pin it in place on the head. Sew in
place. Using green yarn and chain stitch,
embroider a circle around the top of the
headdress (see photograph of shepherd on
page 34 for guidance).

Place the scarf over Joseph's shoulder.
To make the belt, take three lengths of
yarn, approximately 15cm (6in) long, knot
them together at one end and plait them
together. Make a knot at the other end to
secure. Place the belt around Joseph, over
the gown and scarf to check the length,
trim the ends (re-knotting if necessary)
and tie. Secure with a small stitch.

Baby Jesus

Instructions

Techniques

P1B: purl the next stitch together with the corresponding loop from the cast-on edge. This forms the foot shape.

Head

Using pale pink yarn and 2.75mm (UK 12, US 2) knitting needles, cast on 8 sts and purl 1 row.
Next row: (K2, M1) three times, K2 (11 sts).
Next row: (P1, P2tog) three times, P2 (8 sts).
Thread yarn through rem sts and fasten.

Body

Using pale pink yarn and 2.75mm (UK 12, US 2) knitting needles, cast on 8 sts and purl 1 row.
Next row: (K2, M1) three times, K2 (11 sts).
Starting with a purl row, work 5 rows in SS.
Next row: (K1, K2tog) three times, K2 (8 sts).
Thread yarn through rem sts and fasten.

Legs: make two

Using pale pink yarn and 2.75mm (UK 12, US 2) knitting needles, cast on 4 sts and work as follows:
Next row: P3, turn work.
Next row: K2, turn work.
Working just over these centre 2 sts and, starting with a purl row, work 3 rows in SS.
Next row: K to end of row.
Next row: P1, (P1B) twice, P1.
Next row: K1, K2tog, K1 (3 sts).
Starting with a purl row, work 3 rows in SS.
Cast off.

Arms: make two

(The arms can be knitted as an i-cord).
Using pale pink yarn and 2.75mm (UK 12, US 2) knitting needles, cast on 3 sts and work 4 rows in SS.
Thread yarn through rem sts and fasten.

Swaddle

Using cream yarn and 2.75mm (UK 12, US 2) knitting needles, cast on 12 sts and, starting with a knit row, work 6 rows in SS.
Next row: Cast on 4 sts at beg of row, knit to end (16 sts).
Starting with a purl row, work 9 rows in SS.
Next row: (K2tog) eight times (8 sts).
Purl 1 row.
Thread yarn through rem sts and fasten.

Manger

Using brown yarn and 2.75mm (UK 12, US 2) knitting needles, cast on 10 sts and purl 1 row.
Next row: (K1, M1) nine times, K1 (19 sts).
Purl 1 row.
Next row: K4, (M1, K1) four times, K3, (M1, K1) four times, K4 (27 sts).
Purl 1 row.
Next row: (K1, M1) to last st, K1 (53 sts).
Purl 1 row.
Change to 3.25mm (UK 10, US 3) knitting needles and work as follows:
Next row: (K2, P2) to last st, Kfb (54 sts).
Next row: (P2, K2) to last 2 sts, P2.
Next row: (K2, P2) to last 2 sts, K2.
Repeat last 2 rows four more times and then repeat first row once more.
Change to 2.75mm (UK 12, US 2) knitting needles.
Next row: (K2tog) to end of row (27 sts).
Purl 1 row.
Next row: (K1, K2tog) to end of row (18 sts).
Purl 1 row.
Thread yarn through rem sts and fasten.

Materials

4-ply (fingering) yarn in pale pink and cream

Small amount of sportweight (5-ply) yarn in brown

Small amount of yellow 4-ply (fingering) yarn for embroidery

Toy stuffing

Black sewing cotton and sewing needle

2 x black seed beads

Needles

2.75mm (UK 12, US 2) and 3.25mm (UK 10, US 3)

Size

4cm (1½in) high

Making up

Starting at the gathered end of the body, sew the seam up towards the top, filling with a small amount of toy stuffing as you go. The seam goes at the back of the body.

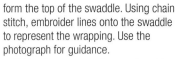

Starting at the gathered end of the head, sew the seam, filling with a small amount of toy stuffing as you go. When you get to the cast-on edge, gather the stitches and fasten.

Taking one of the legs, sew the seam along the back of the leg and each side of the foot. Repeat for the second leg and pin in place on either side of the body. Sew in place, taking the stitching from one side right through the body and out the other side. Repeat this stitch to secure. This will make the legs hinged and able to move.

Sew the seam along the back of the arms, if you have not knitted them as i-cords. Attach the arms to the upper body in the same way as the legs. Embroider a nose with pale pink yarn and a French knot. Using black sewing cotton, sew on the black beads for eyes. Use the photograph for guidance. Sew the cast-on end of the head to the body.

Starting at the gathered end of the swaddle, sew the seam, which will be at the side of the swaddle. Fold the cast-on edge in half and carefully sew together to form the top of the swaddle. Using chain stitch, embroider lines onto the swaddle to represent the wrapping. Use the photograph for guidance.

Taking the manger piece and working from the gathered edge, sew the long side seam, gather the cast-on edge and sew together, making sure that the manger lies flat. Using yellow yarn and straight stitches, embroider the manger to give the appearance of straw. Use the photograph for guidance.

Angel Gabriel

Instructions

Head

Using cream yarn, follow the instructions on page 24.

Body

Using cream yarn, cast on 8 sts and purl 1 row.

Next row: K2, M1, K4, M1, K2 (10 sts).

Next row: P2, M1, P1, M1, P4, M1, P1, M1, P2 (14 sts).

Next row: K3, M1, K1, M1, K6, M1, K1, M1, K3 (18 sts).

Starting with a purl row, work 9 rows in SS.

Next row (RS): Purl (this forms a fold line).

Next row: (P2tog) nine times (9 sts).

Next row: Knit.

Thread yarn through rem sts and fasten.

Gown

Using sparkly white yarn, cast on 10 sts and purl 2 rows.

Next row: K2, M1, K1, M1, K4, M1, K1, M1, K2 (14 sts).

Next row: P3, M1, P1, M1, P6, M1, P1, M1, P3 (18 sts).

Next row: K4, M1, K1, M1, K8, M1, K1, M1, K4 (22 sts).

Purl 1 row.

Next row: K2, (M1, K4) five times (27 sts).

Starting with a purl row, work 3 rows in SS.

Next row: (K3, M1) to last 3 sts, K3 (35 sts).

Starting with a purl row, work 3 rows in SS.

Next row: K2, (K2tog, K3) six times, K2tog, K1 (28 sts).

Next row (WS): Cast off.

Sleeves: make two

Using sparkly white yarn, follow instructions on page 24.

Hands: make two

Using cream yarn, follow the instructions on page 24.

Wings: make two

Using metallic gold yarn, cast on 3 sts and knit 2 rows.

Next row: Cast off 1 st, M1, K1 (3 sts).

Next row: K1, M1, K2 (4 sts).

Next row: K3, M1, K1 (5 sts).

Next row: K1, M1, K2, K2tog (5 sts).

Knit 1 row.

Next row: K1, M1, K4 (6 sts).

Next row: K5, M1, K1 (7 sts).

Next row: K1, M1, K6 (8 sts).

Knit 3 rows.

Next row: Cast off 2 sts, K to end of row (6 sts).

Knit 1 row.

Next row: K1, (K2tog) twice, K1 (4 sts).

Knit 2 rows.

Next row: K1, K2tog, K1 (3 sts).

Knit 1 row.

Next row: sl1, K2tog, psso (1 st).

Fasten off rem st.

Materials

4-ply (fingering) yarn in cream, sparkly white, metallic gold and a small amount of yellow

2 x black seed beads

Black sewing cotton and sewing needle

20cm (8in) of fine wire

PVA glue

Cotton bud and blusher

Toy stuffing

Needles

2.75mm (UK 12, US 2)

Size

6.5cm (2½in) high

Making up

Sew the body together following the instructions on page 26. Sew the head together following the instructions on page 16, attaching the eyes and other features as instructed, and using yellow yarn to embroider the hair with French knots. Follow the instructions on page 26 to sew the head in place. Then add the gown, make the sleeves and attach them. Sew the head to the body, ensuring the seams are towards the back. Lightly press the gown and place on Gabriel. Sew the seam, which will be at the back. Sew the sleeves and hands and attach them to the body, following the instructions for Mary on page 26. Sew the two wings together along the short straight edges, and sew to the back of the gown, using the photograph for guidance. Take the length of fine wire and bend it into a halo shape, leaving a longer piece which will fit inside the back of the gown. Wrap it in metallic gold yarn and secure with a knot. You can paint a dab of PVA glue on the knot to prevent it unravelling. Slide the wire inside the collar of his gown and sew in place to the back of his body under the gown.

Plait three lengths of metallic gold yarn 15cm (6in) long, as for Joseph's belt on page 26. Sew in place round his waist.

Three Kings

Instructions

Head

Using your chosen colour yarn for the head, follow the instructions on page 24.

Body

Using your chosen colour yarn for the body, follow the instructions on page 24. The body will be visible under the gown.

Gown

Using your chosen colour yarn for the gown, follow the instructions on page 24.

Sleeves: make two

Using the same colour yarn used for the gown, follow the instructions on page 24.

Hands: make two

Using your chosen colour for the head, follow the instructions on page 24.

Crown

Using metallic gold yarn, cast on 3 sts and knit 3 rows.
Next row: Cast on 1 st, cast off 1 st, K2 (3 sts).
Knit 3 rows.

Repeat the last 4 rows until the crown, when slightly stretched, fits round the head. Cast off.

Top of the crown

Using the same colour yarn used for the body, cast on 13 sts and purl 1 row.
Next row: K1, M1, (K2, M1) five times, K2 (19 sts).
Starting with a purl row, work 3 rows in SS. Cast off.

Collar

Using your chosen colour yarn for the coat, cast on 10 sts and knit 1 row.
Next row: (K1, M1) to last st, K1 (19 sts).
Knit 2 rows.
Cast off.

Beard

Follow the instructions for Joseph's beard on page 26.

Making up

Sew the head together, following the instructions on page 16, and attaching the eyes and other features as instructed.

Embroider the hair, using dark brown yarn and French knots or straight stitches.

Materials

Small amounts of 4-ply yarn for each king as follows:

King in red gown: cream, dark brown, red and yellow

King in turquoise gown: fawn, dark brown, turquoise and royal blue

King in fuschia gown: fawn, dark brown, fuschia and purple

6 x small black beads

Small amount of metallic gold 4-ply (fingering) yarn

Black sewing cotton and sewing needle

3 x black seed beads

Toy stuffing

Needles

2.75mm (UK 12, US 2)

Size

6.5cm (2½in) high

The top of the crown will cover most of the head. Sew the side seam of the top of the crown and sew in place on top of the king's head. Sew the crown around this, joining cast-on and cast-off edges at the back.

If your king has a beard, sew this in place using the photograph for guidance. If your king has a moustache, embroider the moustache using dark brown yarn and chain stitch or straight stitches. Sew the body together following the instructions on page 26.

Sew the head to the body, ensuring the seams are towards the back. Lightly press the gown and embroider a line around the front edges and the bottom edge using metallic gold yarn and whipped running stitch (see page 19). Place the gown on the king and sew in place around the top edge. Pin the cast-on edge of the collar in place and sew to the top edge of the gown, making sure the edges match the edges of the gown.

Embroider a line around the cast-off edge of the sleeves (the wider edge), using metallic gold yarn and whipped running stitch. Sew the sleeves and hands together and attach to the body, following the instructions for Mary on page 26. Using the same colour yarn used for the hands, sew a decorative bead between the hands, using the photograph for guidance.

Shepherd and Sheep

Instructions

Shepherd's head

Using cream yarn, follow the instructions on page 16.

Body

Using cream yarn, follow the instructions on page 24.

Gown

Using mid-green yarn, follow the instructions on page 24.

Sleeves: make two

Using mid-green yarn, follow the instructions on page 24.

Hands: make two

Using cream yarn, follow the instructions on page 24.

Headdress

Using mid-green yarn, follow the instructions on page 25.

Scarf

Using multicoloured sock yarn, cast on 5 sts and work in GS until work measures 7cm (2¾in). Cast off.

Making up

Sew the body together following the instructions on page 26.

Sew the head together following the instructions on page 16, attaching the eyes and other features as instructed.

Using dark brown yarn, embroider the hair using French knots (see page 19) at the front of the head (the headdress will cover the back). Follow the making-up instructions on page 26 to sew the shepherd together.

For the shepherd's crook, take a 6cm (23/8in) length of fine wire and fold the top over to form the shape of the shepherd's crook, using the photograph for guidance. Wrap brown tweed yarn around the fine wire until it is covered. Place a small dab of PVA glue at either end to secure the yarn and stop it unravelling.

Materials

To make the shepherd:

4-ply (fingering) yarn in cream, fawn, mid-green and a small amount of dark brown and brown tweed

4-ply (fingering) multicoloured sock yarn

PVA glue

2 x 3.4mm (1/8in) black beads

6cm (23/8in) length of fine wire

Toy stuffing

Black sewing cotton and sewing needle

Needles
2.75mm (UK 12, US 2)

Size
6.5cm (2½in) high

Sheep's body

Using a double strand of cream yarn, cast on 22 sts and work the following 4-row pattern.

Row 1: K1, (Kfbf, K3tog) five times, K1.
Row 2: Purl.
Row 3: K1, (K3tog, Kfbf) five times, K1.
Row 4: Purl.

Repeat these 4 rows three more times.

Next row: (K2tog) 11 times (11 sts).

Thread yarn through rem sts, gather and fasten. Leaving a length of yarn long enough to sew the body together.

Head

Using a double strand of cream yarn, cast on 10 sts and knit 1 row.

Next row: K1, M1, K8, M1, K1 (12 sts).

Starting with a purl row, work 3 rows in SS.

Next row: K4, ssK, K2tog, K4 (10 sts).

Next row: P3, ssK, K2tog, P3 (8 sts).

Starting with a knit row, work 3 rows in SS.

Thread yarn through rem sts and fasten.

Legs: make four

Note: The legs can also be worked as an i-cord if preferred.

Using a double strand of cream yarn, cast on 4 sts.

Starting with a knit row, work 3 rows in SS.

Cast off.

Ears: make two

Using a double strand of cream yarn, cast on 3 sts and, starting with a knit row, work 3 rows in SS.

Next row: sl1, P2tog, psso (1 st).

Fasten off rem st.

Tail

Using a double strand of cream yarn, cast on 2 sts and knit 3 rows.

Cast off.

Making up

With the WS on the outside, and starting at the gathered edge, sew the seam of the sheep's body, which will be underneath the sheep. Fill with toy stuffing. Run a length of yarn through the cast-on stitches and gather.

With the WS on the outside and, starting at the gathered edge, sew the seam on the head (this seam will be underneath). The cast-off edge forms the front of the head. Sew the cast-on edges together. This will form the back of the head. Using black sewing cotton, sew the beads in place as eyes. Use the photograph for guidance. Embroider the nose and mouth, using black sewing cotton and straight stitches.

Pin the ears in place on top of the head with the RS towards the back. Sew the ears in place. To give the ears shape, run a length of cream yarn around the outside stitches and pull slightly.

Taking a leg, sew the side seam (if you have not worked an i-cord) and gather the cast-off edge. Repeat for the other three legs. Sew the legs in place, using the photograph for guidance. Sew the tail in place on the back of the sheep.

Lamb's body

Using a double strand of cream yarn, cast on 6 sts and knit 1 row.

Next row: K1, M1, K to last st, M1, K1 (8 sts).

Repeat last row once more (10 sts).

Knit 4 rows.

Next row: K1, K2tog, K to last 3 sts, K2tog, K1 (8 sts).

Repeat last row once more (6 sts).

Thread yarn through rem sts and fasten.

Head

Using a double strand of cream yarn, cast on 6 sts and purl 1 row.

Next row: K1, M1, K to last st, M1, K1 (8 sts).

Starting with a purl row work 3 rows in SS.

Next row: (K2tog) four times (4 sts).
Thread yarn through rem sts and gather.

Legs

Note: The legs can also be worked as an i-cord if preferred.

Using a double strand of cream yarn, cast on 4 sts and, starting with a knit row, work 4 rows in SS.

Thread yarn through rem sts, pull tightly and fasten.

Ears

Using a double strand of cream yarn, cast on 2 sts.
Knit 2 rows.
Next row: K2tog (1 st).
Fasten off rem st.

Tail

Using a double strand of cream yarn, cast on 2 sts.
Knit 3 rows.
Next row: K2tog (1 st).
Fasten off rem st.

Making up

Starting at the gathered edge, sew the seam of the lamb's body, which will be underneath the lamb. Fill with toy stuffing. Run a length of yarn through the cast-on stitches and gather.

With the WS on the outside, sew the seam on the head (this will be underneath) from the gathered edge. This edge forms the front of the head. Sew the cast-on edges together. This will form the back of the head. Using black sewing cotton, embroider two eyes using French knots (see page 19). Embroider the nose and mouth, using black sewing cotton and straight stitches.

Pin the ears in place on top of the head and sew the ears in place. To give the ears shape, run a length of cream yarn around the outside stitches and pull slightly.

Taking a leg, sew the side seam and gather the cast-off edge. Repeat for the other three legs. Sew the legs in place, using the photograph for guidance. Sew the tail in place on the back of the lamb.

Little Donkey

Instructions

Note: For the wrap and turn (w&t) technique, see page 12.

Head and body

Using cream (contrast colour) yarn, cast on 7 sts and purl 1 row.

Next row: (K1, M1) twice, K2, (M1, K1) three times (12 sts).

Purl 1 row.

Join in grey (main colour) yarn.

From now on, work all sts marked as MC using main colour yarn and all sts marked as CC using contrast colour yarn.

Next row: K5MC, K2CC, K5MC.

Next row: P5MC, P2CC, P5MC.

Next row: K5MC, K2CC, K5MC.

Break off the cream (contrast colour) yarn. You will now be working using the grey (main colour) yarn only.

Starting with a purl row, work 2 rows in SS.

Work the following rows using the wrap and turn technique and picking up the 'wraps' on the following row (see page 12). This gives a neat finish. This section will form the top of the donkey's head.

Next row: P7, w&t.

Next row: K2, w&t.

Next row: P3, w&t.

Next row: K4, w&t.

Next row: P5, w&t.

Next row: K6, w&t.

Next row: P7, w&t.

Next row: Knit to end of row.

Starting with a purl row, work 3 rows in SS.

Next row: K1, M1, K to last st, M1, K1 (14 sts).

Purl 1 row.

Next row: K3, cast off 8 sts, K2 (leaving two groups of 3 sts).

Cast on 4 sts, P7, turn work, cast on 4 sts, turn work, purl to end of row (14 sts).

Next row: Cast on 4 sts and K to end of row (18 sts).

Next row: P1, M1, P to last st, M1, P1 (20 sts).

Next row: K1, M1, K to last st, M1, K1 (22 sts).

Starting with a purl row, work 13 rows in SS.

Next row: K1, ssK, K to last 3 sts, K2tog, K1 (20 sts).

Purl 1 row.

Next row: K1, ssK, K5, ssK, K2tog, K5, K2tog, K1 (16 sts).

Purl 1 row.

Cast off using the three-needle cast-off technique (see page 21).

Ears: make two

Using grey yarn, cast on 5 sts and, starting with a knit row, work 4 rows in SS.

Next row: ssK, K1, K2tog (3 sts).

Purl 1 row.

Materials

4-ply (fingering) yarn in grey (main colour), cream (contrast colour) and black

Self-patterning 4-ply (fingering) sock yarn

Toy stuffing

2 x 3.4mm (⅛in) black beads

2 x chenille sticks

Black sewing cotton and sewing needle

Needles

2.75mm (UK 12, US 2)

Crochet hook (optional)

Size

7cm (2¾in) high

Next row: sl1, K2tog, psso (1 st).

Fasten off rem st.

Tail

Using grey yarn, cast on 5 sts and, starting with a knit row, work 8 rows in SS.

Cast off.

Legs: make four

Using black yarn, cast on 7 sts and, starting with a knit row, work 2 rows in SS.

Change to grey yarn and, starting with a knit row, work 8 rows in SS.

Cast off.

Blanket

Using self-patterning 4-ply (fingering) sock yarn, cast on 12 sts and knit 1 row.

Next row: sl1, K to end of row.

Repeat the last row until the blanket measures 7cm (2¾in).

Cast off.

Making up

Following the instructions on page 14, sew your donkey together. With the wrong side of the ears facing forward, pin each ear in place on top of the head, using the photograph for guidance, and sew in place. Sew the black beads in place for the eyes. Using black sewing cotton, embroider the mouth using straight sts.

Take four lengths of black yarn, approximately 10cm (4in) long and knot them together at one end. Place the knot inside the tail. Sew the side seam of the tail, making sure the black yarn knot is secured inside. Trim the lengths of black yarn to form the tassel at the end of the tail. Use the photograph for guidance.

Taking the black yarn, sew loops onto the donkey's neck and between the ears. Using black yarn, work small stitches along each side of the mane to secure the loops you have made at the edges. Cut the loops open and trim the mane into shape.

Make tassels for the blanket by folding a piece of matching yarn in half and looping it through the cast-on edge using a small crochet hook, or thread the looped yarn onto a needle to pull it through. Pull

the end of the yarn through the loop to secure to the blanket.

Make loops all along the side of the blanket, using the photograph for guidance. Repeat for the cast-off edge of the blanket. Trim to length.

Place the blanket on the donkey and sew the front corners of the bottom edge together, making sure that the blanket will still slide over the donkey's head.

Shooting Star

Instructions

Note: A double strand of 2-ply (laceweight) yarn, used for the gold star, is equivalent to a single strand of 4-ply (fingering) yarn (used for the sparkly white star). For the wrap and turn (w&t) technique, see page 12.

Star: make two

Using a double strand of gold yarn, cast on 2 sts and purl 1 row.
Next row: K1, M1, K1 (3 sts).
Purl 1 row.
Next row: (K1, M1) twice, K1 (5 sts).
Starting with a purl row, work 2 rows in SS.
Place sts on a holder or spare needle.
Make another four 'points' in the same way, sliding each one onto the stitch holder or spare needle.
With WS facing, purl across the sts from all five points (25 sts).
Next row: (K1, K2tog) eight times, K1 (17 sts).
Purl 1 row.
Next row: (K2tog) eight times, K1 (9 sts).
Thread yarn through rem sts leaving a length of yarn for sewing up.

Star tail

Using a double strand of gold yarn, cast on 6 sts and, starting with a knit row, work 2 rows in SS.
Next row: K5, M1, K1 (7 sts).
Next row: P1, M1, P6 (8 sts).
Next row: K7, M1, K1 (9 sts).
Next row: P1, M1, P5, P2togtbl, P1 (9 sts).
Starting with a knit row, work 2 rows in SS.
Next row: K1, ssK, K5, M1, K1 (9 sts).
Purl 1 row.
Next row: K to last st, M1, K1 (10 sts).
Starting with a purl row, work 3 rows in SS.
Repeat last 4 rows once more (11 sts).
Next row: K1, M1, K7, K2tog, K1 (11 sts).

Next row: P1, P2tog, P8 (10 sts).
Knit 1 row.
Next row: P6, w&t.
Next row: K to end of row.
Next row: P4, w&t.
Next row: K to end of row.
Next row: (P1, P2tog, YO) twice, P1, P2tog, P1 (9 sts).
Next row: K8, M1, K1 (10 sts).
Next row: P4, w&t.
Next row: K to end of row.
Next row: P6, w&t.
Next row: K to end of row.
Next row: P1, M1, P9 (11 sts).
Next row: K1, ssK, K7, M1, K1 (11 sts).
Starting with a purl row, work 3 rows in SS.
Repeat last 4 rows once more.
Next row: K1, ssK, K5, K2tog, K1 (9 sts).
Next row: P1, P2tog, P6 (8 sts).
Starting with a knit row, work 4 rows in SS.
Next row: K5, K2tog, K1 (7 sts).
Purl 1 row.
Next row: K4, K2tog, K1 (6 sts).
Starting with a purl row, work 3 rows in SS.
Cast off.

Making up

With WS together, sew the two star pieces carefully together, hiding all the loose ends inside the star and lightly filling with toy stuffing as you go. Leave two points of the star unsewn. Fold the tail of the star in half with WS together and sew the side seams, filling with a small amount of toy stuffing to add definition. Sew a stitch where each 'yarn over' is (on the fold), to define the picot edge. Using backstitch, embroider a curved line from each of these stitches to the end of the tail, using the photograph for guidance. Slide the end of the tail into the star where you have left it unsewn. Pin in place.

When you are happy with the position of the tail, sew each side of the star to the tail, placing a tiny amount of toy stuffing inside each point. Taking a length of metallic gold yarn approximately 15cm (6in) long, sew one end to the tail and the other end to a point on the star so that you can hang the star up. Use the photograph for guidance.

Materials

2-ply (laceweight) yarn in gold (use a double strand throughout)

15cm (6in) of 4-ply (fingering) yarn in metallic gold

Make a second star using a single strand of 4-ply (fingering) yarn in sparkly white

Toy stuffing

Needles

2.75mm (UK 12, US 2)
Stitch holder or spare needle

Size

Each star is approximately 10cm (4in) long

Stable

Instructions

Stable

Note: This project uses the Shooting Star pattern on page 40.

Stripe pattern

Row 1: Knit (WS).
Row 2: Knit all sts.
Row 3: Purl all sts.
Row 4: Knit all sts.

Roof tile pattern

Row 1: Knit (WS).
Row 2: (K3, sl1) to last 2 sts, K2.
Row 3: P2, (sl1, P3) to end of row.
Row 4: (K3, sl1) to last 2 sts, K2.
Row 5: Knit (WS).
Row 6: K1, sl1, (K3, sl1) to end of row.
Row 7: (sl1, P3) to last 2 sts, sl1, P1.
Row 8: K1, sl1, (K3, sl1) to end of row.

Base

Using brown tweed yarn, cast on 36 sts and, starting with a knit row, work in SS until work measures 7cm (2¾in), ending with a purl row.
Next row: Purl 1 row (this creates a fold line).
Starting with a purl row, work 7cm (2¾in) in SS.
Cast off.

Sides: make four pieces

Using Tweed brown yarn cast on 22 sts and work in stripe pattern until work measures 8.5cm (3³⁄₈in).
Cast off.

Back and front: make four pieces

Using brown tweed yarn and cast on 36 sts and work in stripe pattern until work measures 8.5cm (3³⁄₈in), ending with a WS row. You will now be decreasing at each end of every row for the slope of the roof.

Next row: K1, ssK, K to last 3 sts, K2tog, K1.
Next row: P1, P2tog, P to last 3 sts, P2togtbl, P1.
Work these 2 rows until 4 sts remain.
Next row: SsK, K2tog (2 sts).
Thread yarn through rem sts and fasten.

Rooftops

Outside pieces: make two

Using stone tweed yarn, cast on 26 sts and work roof tile pattern until work measures 9.5cm (3¾in).
Cast off.

Inside pieces: make two

Using stone tweed yarn, cast on 26 sts and, starting with a knit row, work in SS until work measures 9.5cm (3¾in).
Cast off.

Shooting Star

Using a single strand of yellow yarn, follow the instructions for the Shooting Star on pages 40–41.

Making up

Using an iron, lightly and gently steam all pieces to size. Cut the cardboard pieces out using the measurements (see right) and the template on page 13. With RS on the outside, fold the base piece around the cardboard and sew around the edges to encase the cardboard. For the stable side, front and back, place the card inside the two knitted pieces with the RS on the outside and sew around the edges. Repeat for the roof sections using one rooftop piece and one inside piece for each side.

Sew the back of the stable to the base along the bottom edge. Sew the two side sections in place in the same way. Sew the side seams to join to the back of the stable.

Place the two rooftop sections together, so that the cast-on edges are in the centre. Sew them together.

Materials

180m (197yds) of 4-ply (fingering) yarn in brown tweed

90m (98½yds) of 4-ply (fingering) yarn in stone tweed

4-ply (fingering) yarn in yellow

Small amount of dark brown 4-ply (fingering) yarn for embroidery

Toy stuffing

2 x small brown buttons

Brown sewing cotton and sewing needle

2 x A4 sheets of thick cardboard

20cm (8in) length of fine wire

Needles

2.75mm (UK12, US2)

Size

14cm (5½in) from base to apex of the roof, 8cm (3¹⁄₈in) deep and 15cm (6in) wide

Each piece measures:

Base: 14cm (5½in) wide x 7cm (2¾in) long

Sides: 8.5cm (3³⁄₈in) high x 7cm (2¾in) wide

Back and front: 14cm (5½in) wide x 8.5cm (3³⁄₈in) high, sloping up to 12.5cm (5in) high to top of pitch

Roof: 9.5cm (3¾in) long x 8.5cm (3³⁄₈in) wide

Place the roof on top of the stable and sew to the side sections and the back, using the photograph for guidance. Sew the front of the stable to the base, ensuring it works as a 'hinge'. Sew the two buttons in place, using the photograph for guidance, at the top front edge of the stable (see also page 23 for a photograph of the stable with the front open).

Make two loops as follows: Cast on 1 stitch. Knit the stitch, leaving the resulting stitch on the right-hand needle. Repeat this process until you have a 'chain' long enough to loop over the button. Sew a loop to each side of the stable front to correspond with each button. Using dark brown yarn, embroider the doors onto the front section of the stable, using the photograph for guidance. Sew the star to the top of the stable, sliding a length of fine wire inside the star and down inside the roof section to help it stand up.

Christmas Projects

Santa Claus

Instructions

Note: For the wrap and turn (w&t) technique, see page 12.

Head

Using pale pink yarn yarn, cast on 13 sts and purl 1 row.

Next row: K1, M1, (K2, M1) five times, K2 (19 sts).

Starting with a purl row, work 3 rows in SS.

Next row: K9, Kfb, turn.

Next row: P2, turn.

Next row: K to end of row.

Next row: P9, P2tog, P9 (19 sts).

Next row: K5, (ssK) twice, K1, (K2tog) twice, K5 (15 sts).

Starting with a purl row, work 3 rows in SS.

Next row: K1, K2tog, K2, K2tog, K1, K2tog, K2, K2tog, K1 (11 sts).

Thread yarn through rem sts and fasten.

Body

Using red yarn, cast on 10 sts and purl 1 row.

Next row: K2, M1, K1, M1, K4, M1, K1, M1, K2 (14 sts).

Next row: P3, M1, P1, M1, P6, M1, P1, M1, P3 (18 sts).

Next row: K4, M1, K1, M1, K8, M1, K1, M1, K4 (22 sts).

Purl 1 row.

Next row: (K3, M1) six times, K4 (28 sts).

Starting with a purl row, work 9 rows in SS.

Next row (RS): Purl (this forms a fold line).

Next row: (P2tog) fourteen times (14 sts).

Starting with a knit row, work 2 rows in SS.

Next row: (K2tog) seven times (7 sts).

Thread yarn through rem sts and fasten.

Lower edge body trim

Using sparkly white yarn, cast on 26 sts and knit 3 rows.

Cast off.

Front band

Using sparkly white yarn, cast on 3 sts and work in GS until band is long enough to reach from top to bottom edge of body. Cast off.

Belt

Using black yarn, cast on 3 sts and, starting with a knit row, work in SS until belt, when slightly stretched, is long enough to fit around middle of body. Cast off.

Bobble hat

Using sparkly white yarn, cast on 20 sts and knit 3 rows.

Change to red yarn and, starting with a knit row, work 6 rows in SS.

Next row: K9, w&t.

Next row: P5, w&t.

Next row: K to end of row.

Next row: (P2, P2tog) five times (15 sts).

Materials

4-ply (fingering) yarn in pale pink, red, sparkly white, black, and white angora

20cm (8in) of 4-ply (fingering) yarn in metallic gold

2 x 3.4mm (¹⁄₈in) black beads

Toy stuffing

Black sewing cotton and sewing needle

Needles

2.75mm (UK 12, US 2)

Size

10cm (4in) high

Next row: K6, w&t.

Next row: P to end of row.

Next row: K8, K2tog, K1, K2tog, K2 (13 sts).

Purl 1 row.

Next row: (K1, K2tog) four times, K1 (9 sts).

Purl 1 row.

Thread yarn through rem sts and fasten.

Hat bobble

Note: The bobble is worked in SS and the WS will be on the outside when sewn up.
Using sparkly white yarn, cast on 3 sts.
Next row: (K1, M1) twice, K1 (5 sts).
Starting with a purl row, work 3 rows in SS.
Next row: K2tog, K1, K2tog (3 sts).
Thread yarn through rem sts.

Sleeves: make two

Using red yarn, cast on 8 sts and, starting with a knit row, work two rows in SS.
Next row: K1, M1, K6, M1, K1 (10 sts).
Starting with a purl row, work 5 rows in SS.
Change to sparkly white yarn and knit 4 rows.
Cast off.

Gloves: make two

Using black yarn, cast on 4 sts and, starting with a knit row, work 8 rows in SS.
Cast off.

Legs: make two

Using red yarn, cast on 8 sts and, starting with a knit row, work 2 rows in SS.
Next row: K1, M1, K6, M1, K1 (10 sts).
Starting with a purl row, work 3 rows in SS.
Change to sparkly white yarn and knit 4 rows.
Cast off.

Boots: make two

Using black yarn, cast on 12 sts and, starting with a knit row, work 3 rows in SS.
Next row: P4, P2tog, P2togtbl, P4 (10 sts).
Next row: K3, ssK, K2tog, K3 (8 sts).
Next row: P2, P2tog, P2togtbl, P2 (6 sts).
Starting with a knit row, work 2 rows in SS.
Cast off.

Beard

Using white angora yarn, cast on 3 sts and purl 1 row.
Next row: (K1, M1) twice, K1 (5 sts).
Purl 1 row.
Next row: K1, M1, K3, M1, K1 (7 sts).
Next row: Cast on 3 sts, cast off 9 sts (1 st).
Next row: Cast on 3 sts, cast off all sts (1 st).
Fasten off rem st.

Making up

Starting at the gathered cast-off edge of the body, sew the side seam, filling with toy stuffing as you go. Gather the cast-on edge, tighten and secure. Carefully sew the front band and lower edge body trim in place, making sure it overlaps the bottom edge of the body slightly. Sew the black belt around the middle of the body, catching the cast-on and cast-off edges together at the back of the body. Using the photograph for guidance, embroider the buckle using metallic gold yarn and straight stitches.

Sew the head together using the instructions on pages 16–17, adding eyes and blusher as instructed.

Using sparkly white yarn, sew the band of the hat together, change to red yarn and sew the remainder of the seam. With the WS on the outside, run a gathering yarn around the outside edge of the bobble, using the length of yarn left at the end of the bobble. Place a tiny amount of toy stuffing inside, then pull up and secure. Sew firmly to the top of the hat. Place the hat on the head using the photograph as guidance and sew in place. Taking the beard, sew either side

to the edge of the hat. Embroider the moustache using white angora yarn and straight stitches.

Taking one glove, fold it in half with the WS together, so that the cast-on and cast-off edges are together, and sew the seams. Sew the glove to the inside of the cast-off edge of the sleeve using the sparkly white yarn so that the stitches do not show on the outside of the sleeve.

Repeat for the second glove and sleeve.

Note: Sew one glove to the left of the cast-off edge and the other to the right. When sewing the sleeves to the body, make sure the side the glove is sewn to is against the body. Sew the sleeve seams and pin each arm in place towards the back of the body, using the photograph for guidance. Sew the sleeves in place.

Sew the head to the body, ensuring the seams of the head and body are towards the back.

Taking one of the boots, sew the cast-on edge together; this will form the bottom of the boot. Sew the back seam and the cast-off stitches, filling the boot with a small amount of toy stuffing. Repeat for the second boot.

Taking one of the legs and starting at the cast-on edge, sew the seam using red yarn, and sew the bottom of the leg together using sparkly white yarn. Sew the boot to the bottom edge of the leg, making sure that the seam is towards the back of the leg. Repeat for the second leg. Sew each leg in place at the front of the bottom of the body.

Sleigh

Instructions

Base of sleigh

The base is knitted in one piece. Using brown tweed yarn, cast on 20 sts and, starting with a knit row, work in SS until work measures 16.5cm (6½in), ending with a purl row.
Next row (RS): Purl (this forms a fold line).
Starting with a purl row, work in SS until work measures 16.5cm (6½in) from fold line, ending with a purl row.
Cast off.

Right sleigh side: make two

Using brown tweed yarn, cast on 5 sts and purl 1 row.
Next row: K1, M1, K3, M1, K1 (7 sts).
Next row: P1, M1, P5, M1, P1 (9 sts).
Next row: K1, M1, K7, M1, K1 (11 sts).
Starting with a purl row, work 2 rows in SS.
Next row: Cast off 2 sts, purl to end of row (9 sts).
Knit 1 row.
Next row: Cast off 1 st, purl to end of row (8 sts).
Starting with a knit row, work 10 rows in SS.
Next row: K5, K2tog, K1 (7 sts).
Starting with a purl row, work 10 rows in SS.
Next row: P1, M1, P6 (8 sts).
Knit 1 row.

Next row: P1, M1, P7 (9 sts).
Knit 1 row.
Next row: P1, M1, P5, P2tog, P1 (9 sts).
Knit 1 row.
Repeat last 2 rows once more.
Next row: P1, M1, P5, P2tog, P1 (9 sts).
Next row: K1, ssK, K6 (8 sts).
Purl 1 row.
Cast off.

Left sleigh side: make two

Using brown tweed yarn, cast on 5 sts and purl 1 row.
Next row: K1, M1, K3, M1, K1 (7 sts).
Next row: P1, M1, P5, M1, P1 (9 sts).
Next row: K1, M1, K7, M1, K1 (11 sts).
Starting with a purl row, work 3 rows in SS.
Next row: Cast off 2 sts, knit to end of row (9 sts).
Purl 1 row.
Next row: Cast off 1 st, knit to end of row (8 sts).
Starting with a purl row, work 9 rows in SS.
Next row: K1, ssK, K5 (7 sts).
Starting with a purl row, work 10 rows in SS.
Next row: P6, M1, P1 (8 sts).
Knit 1 row.
Next row: P7, M1, P1 (9 sts).

Materials

90m (98½yd) of 4-ply (fingering) yarn in brown tweed
4-ply (fingering) yarn in metallic gold and green
2m (2¼yd) of red 4-ply (fingering) yarn for cord reins
3 x 4mm (³/₁₆in) red beads
2 x chenille sticks at least 20cm (8in) long
Thick cardboard 16.5 x 6.5cm (6½ x 2½in) piece of heavyweight sew-in interfacing or thin card

Needles

2.75mm (UK 12, US 2)

Size

12cm (4¾in) long

Knit 1 row.
Next row: P1, P2tog, P5, M1, P1 (9 sts).
Knit 1 row.
Repeat last 2 rows once more.
Next row: P1, P2tog, P5, M1, P1 (9 sts).
Next row: K6, ssK, K1 (8 sts).
Purl 1 row.
Cast off.

Note: Before knitting the sleigh runners, sew the sleigh together following the instructions on page 52. Using the photographs for guidance, shape two chenille sticks to form the runners.

Sleigh runners: make two

Using metallic gold yarn, cast on 7 sts and work in SS until work is long enough to cover the chenille stick.

Cast off.

Holly leaves: make two

Using green yarn, cast on 2 sts and purl 1 row.

Next row: Kfb, YO, Kfb (5 sts).

Purl 1 row.

Next row: Cast off 1 st, knit to end of row (4 sts).

Next row: Cast off 1 st, purl to end of row (3 sts).

Next row: Kfb, K1, Kfb (5 sts).

Purl 1 row.

Next row: Cast off 2 sts, knit to end of row (3 sts).

Next row: Cast off 2 sts, purl to end of row (1 st).

Thread yarn through rem st and fasten.

Making up

Lightly press the base and sleigh sides to lessen the curling and make them easier to sew together. Using the template for the sleigh sides (see below), cut two sleigh sides from thick cardboard. Taking one right and one left knitted sleigh side, sew them together around the cardboard, with the RS facing outwards. Repeat for the second side.

Taking the sleigh base, fold in half with WS together along the fold line. Sew along one side (long edge) and the end opposite the fold line. Slide the interfacing (or thin card) inside the sleigh base and then sew the remaining seam to enclose it.

Pin the base to the sleigh sides along the inside edge and sew firmly in place. Shape the chenille sticks as shown in the photographs to make the sleigh runners.

Sew one runner around one chenille stick, keeping the chenille stick as already shaped. Repeat for the second runner. Using the photograph for guidance, pin the runners in place close to the edge of the sleigh. Sew firmly in place to the base. Stitch the curled front edge of the runner to the front slope of the sleigh, using the photograph for guidance.

Using chain stitch (see page 18) and metallic gold yarn, embroider the markings on the sides, front and back of the sleigh. If you find it easier, use some sewing cotton in a contrasting colour and sew a line in running stitch as a guide. Work the chain stitch following the line and then pull out the sewing cotton.

Sew two holly leaves to the front of the sleigh, using the photograph for guidance, and use green yarn to sew the beads in place.

To make the red cord reins, place the reindeer and sleigh in a line and measure from the front of Rudolph to the back of the sleigh. Take this measurement and multiply it by four. Cut a length of red yarn to this length. Knot one end around something to secure it (I used a door handle) and twist in the same direction of the twist of the yarn until it starts to twist back on itself. Allow it to twist and you will end up with a cord. Knot each end and thread through the gold loops on the reindeer collars, placing each end in the sleigh.

Template for Sleigh side: 100%

Reindeer

Instructions

Note: For the wrap and turn (w&t) technique, see page 12.

Head and body

Using brown hand-dyed yarn, cast on 7 sts and purl 1 row.

Next row: (K1, M1) twice, K2, (M1, K1). three times (12 sts).

Starting with a purl row, work 6 rows in SS.

Next row: P7, w&t.

Next row: K2, w&t.

Next row: P3, w&t.

Next row: K4, w&t.

Next row: P5, w&t.

Next row: K6, w&t.

Next row: P7, w&t.

Next row: Knit to end of row.

Starting with a purl row, work 3 rows in SS.

Next row: K1, M1, K to last st, M1, K1 (14 sts).

Purl 1 row.

Next row: K3, cast off 8 sts, K2, leaving two groups of 3 sts.

Next row: Cast on 4 sts, P7, turn work and cast on 4 sts, turn work and P to end of row (14 sts).

Next row: Cast on 4 sts and knit to end of row (18 sts).

Next row: P1, M1, P to last st, M1, P1 (20 sts).

Next row: K1, M1, K to last st, M1, K1 (22 sts).

Starting with a purl row, work 13 rows in SS.

Next row: K1, ssK, knit to last 3 sts, K2tog, K1 (20 sts).

Purl 1 row.

Next row: K1, ssK, K5, ssK, K2tog, K5, K2tog, K1 (16 sts).

Purl 1 row.

Divide the 16 rem sts between two needles and, with RS together and using a third

needle, cast off using the three-needle cast-off technique (see page 21).

Ears: make two

Using dark brown hand-dyed yarn cast on 4 sts and, starting with a knit row, work 2 rows in SS.

Next row: ssK, K2tog (2 sts).

Next row: P2tog (1 st).

Fasten off rem st.

Antlers: make two

Using dark brown yarn cast on 8 sts.

Next row: Cast off 4 sts.

Sl st back to left-hand needle (4 sts).

Next row: Cast on 3 sts, cast off 4 sts.

Sl st back to left-hand needle (3 sts).

Next row: Cast on 3 sts, cast off rem sts.

Fasten off rem st.

Materials

- Hand-dyed 4-ply (fingering) yarn in brown
- 4-ply (fingering) yarn in dark brown, red, black and metallic gold
- Small amount of orange 4-ply (fingering) yarn and green 2-ply (laceweight) yarn
- 2 x 3.4mm ($1/8$in) black beads per reindeer
- 2 x 8mm ($5/16$in) gold-coloured jump rings per reindeer
- 1 x 5mm ($3/16$in) brass bell (for Rudolph)
- Black sewing cotton and sewing needle
- Toy stuffing

Needles
2.75mm (UK 12, US 2)

Size
6.5cm (2½in) tall and 8cm (3$1/8$in) from nose to tail

Tail

Using dark brown hand-dyed yarn, cast on 3 sts and work 3 rows in SS.
Next row: sl1, K2tog, psso, (1 st).
Fasten off rem st.

Legs: make four

Using dark brown yarn, cast on 7 sts and, starting with a knit row, work 2 rows in SS. Change to dark brown hand-dyed yarn and, starting with a knit row, work 8 rows in SS.
Cast off.

Collar

Using metallic gold yarn, cast on 22 sts. Change to red yarn and, starting with a knit row, work 4 rows in SS. Change to metallic gold yarn and cast off.

Tip: Do not cut the gold yarn when you change to red, just carry the yarn up the side of your work and use the same strand to cast off. That will cut down on the number of ends to darn in.

Carrot

Using orange yarn, cast on 1 st.
Next row: Kfbf (3 sts).
Purl 1 row.
Next row: (K1, M1) three times, K1 (7 sts).
Purl 1 row.
Thread yarn through rem sts, leaving a length of yarn for sewing up.

Carrot top: make two

Using green yarn, cast on 6 sts and cast off 3 sts.
Slip the resulting st back to the left-hand needle (3 sts).
Cast on 3 sts, cast off all sts.
Fasten off rem stitch.

Nose: Rudolph only

Using red yarn, cast on 1 st.
Next row: Kfbf (3 sts).
Knit 1 row.
Next row: sl1, P2tog, psso (1 st).
Fasten off rem st.

Making up

Follow instructions on page 14 to sew your reindeer together. Using the photographs for guidance, pin each ear in place on top of the head with the WS facing forwards and sew in place.

Sew two antlers in place between the ears on the top of the head, making sure that they are symmetrical. Sew the beads in place for the eyes. Using black yarn, embroider a French knot for a nose and then embroider a mouth using straight stitches. For Rudolph, run a line of stitches around the outside edge of the nose, gather to form a ball and secure. Sew the nose in place and then embroider a mouth using the black yarn. Sew the tail in place at the top of the back seam.

Taking the collar, place it around the reindeer's neck with the tighter edge (in my case, this was the cast-on edge)

towards the top. Sew the short edges together at the front of the neck as shown in the photographs. Using metallic gold yarn, sew the collar on along the cast-on and cast-off edges. Using red yarn, sew a gold ring on either side of the collar using the photograph for guidance. For Rudolph, add a small brass bell at the front top edge of the collar and a third ring below it.

Using orange yarn, sew the side seam of the carrot. Thread the yarn back up to the top of the carrot, then down to the base of the carrot, tighten and secure. This gives the top of the carrot a good shape. Carefully sew the carrot tops in place, threading the yarn down through the carrot and securing so that it does not show. To make the reins, see the making up instructions for the Sleigh on page 52.

Mini Gifts

Instructions

Large gift

Using your chosen colour yarn, cast on 8 sts and, starting with a knit row, work 6 rows in SS.

Next row (RS): Purl 1 row (this forms a fold line).

Next row: Cast on 5 sts, purl to end of row (13 sts).

Next row: Cast on 13 sts and work as follows:

K7, sl1, K5, sl1, K7, sl1, K4 (26 sts).

Purl 1 row.

Next row: K7, sl1, K5, sl1, K7, sl1, K4.

Purl 1 row.

Repeat the last 2 rows two more times.

Next row: Cast off 13 sts, P7, K5 (13 sts).

Next row: Cast off 5 sts, purl to end of row (8 sts).

Starting with a knit row, work 5 rows in SS.

Cast off.

Small gift

Using your chosen colour yarn, cast on 6 sts and, starting with a knit row, work 6 rows in SS.

Next row: Cast on 5 sts, K5, P6 (11 sts). This forms a fold line.

Next row: Cast on 11 sts and purl to end of row (22 sts).

Next row: (K5, sl1) three times, K4.

Purl 1 row.

Repeat the last 2 rows twice more.

Next row: Cast off 5 sts, P5, K11 (17 sts).

Next row: Cast off 11 sts, purl to end of row (6 sts).

Starting with a knit row, work 5 rows in SS.

Cast off.

Making up

Lightly press the gifts to lessen the curling and make them easier to sew together. Sew each gift into a 'cube' shape, filling with toy stuffing as you go. Using metallic gold yarn, embroider a 'ribbon' in chain stitch, as shown in the photographs.

Materials

4-ply (fingering) yarn in yellow, fuchsia, green, turquoise, purple and metallic gold

Toy stuffing

Needles
2.75mm (UK 12, US 2)

Size
Small gift: 2 x 2cm (¾ x ¾in)

Large gift: 2 x 3cm (¾ x 1¼in)

Mistletoe

Instructions

Leaves: make two per stem

Using green yarn, cast on 4 sts and purl 1 row.

Next row: K2, M1, K2 (5 sts).

Purl 1 row.

Next row: K1, M1, K3, M1, K1 (7 sts).

Starting with a purl row, work 5 rows in SS.

Next row: K1, ssK, K1, K2tog, K1 (5 sts).

Purl 1 row.

Next row: K1, ssK, K2 (4 sts).

Purl 1 row.

Next row: K1, K2tog, K1 (3 sts).

Purl 1 row.*

Place the finished leaf on a stitch holder or spare knitting needle and knit a second leaf. Place both leaves on a knitting needle and, with RS facing, work as follows across the 6 sts:

K2, K2tog, K2 (5 sts).

Continue on these 5 sts working an i-cord (see page 20) for 6cm (23/8in). Thread yarn through rem sts, gather and fasten.

Note: If you would prefer not to use the i-cord technique, work in SS and then sew the seam at the back of the stem together.

Make two more leaves without stems, following the instructions to *.

Finish each leaf as follows:

Next row: sl1, K2tog, psso (1 st).

Fasten off rem st.

Berries: make two per sprig

Using cream yarn, cast on 2 sts and purl 1 row.

Next row: (Kfb) twice (4 sts).

Starting with a purl row, work 3 rows in SS.

Next row: (K2tog) twice (2 sts).

Thread yarn through rem sts and fasten.

Making up

With WS together, pin a leaf without a stem to the back of each leaf with a stem. Taking a chenille stick, slide one end up the stem and make a 'loop' to fit inside one leaf. Repeat for the second leaf. Sew each leaf together, hiding the chenille stick inside.

Taking a berry, run a length of yarn around the outside edge and gather into a berry shape, placing a small amount of toy stuffing inside. Repeat for the second berry and sew in place, using the photograph for guidance.

Make three sprigs in total and tie green yarn around the stems to secure. Make a loop of satin cord, knot and loop around the sprigs of misletoe.

Materials

4-ply (fingering) yarn in green and cream

1 x 36cm (14in) length of red satin cord

Stitch holder or spare knitting needle

Chenille sticks

Toy stuffing

Needles

2.75mm (UK 12, US 2), double-pointed if you are using the i-cord technique

Size

Each leaf is approx. 3.5cm (1³/₈in) long

Penguins

Materials

4-ply (fingering) yarn in sparkly white, black, yellow, red and green

Make a second penguin using sparkly white, grey, yellow, pink and cream

2 x 3.4mm (1/8in) black beads

Toy stuffing

Needles
2.75mm (UK 12, US 2)

Size
8cm (3 1/8in) high

Instructions

Body

Using sparkly white yarn, cast on 13 sts and purl 1 row.

Next row: K1, M1, (K2, M1) five times, K2 (19 sts).

Starting with a purl row, work 5 rows in SS.

Next row: (K3, M1) five times, K4 (24 sts).

Purl 1 row.

Next row: (K3, M1) seven times, K3 (31 sts).

Starting with a purl row, work 5 rows in SS.

Next row: K10, M1, (K3, M1) four times, K9 (36 sts).

Starting with a purl row, work 9 rows in SS.

Next row: (K3, K2tog) seven times, K1 (29 sts).

Purl 1 row.

Next row: (K2, K2tog) seven times, K1 (22 sts).

Purl 1 row.

Continuing in SS, cast off 8 sts at the beginning of the next 2 rows (6 sts).

Next row: K1, M1, K4, M1, K1 (8 sts).

Starting with a purl row, work 3 rows in SS.

Next row: K1, ssK, K2, K2tog, K1 (6 sts).

Purl 1 row.

Next row: K1, ssK, K2tog, K1 (4 sts).

Cast off.

Outer body

Using black yarn, cast on 13 sts and purl 1 row.

Next row: K1, M1, (K2, M1) five times, K2 (19 sts).

Purl 1 row.

Continuing in SS, cast off 2 sts at the beginning of the next 2 rows (15 sts).

Starting with a knit row, work 2 rows in SS.

Next row: K1, M1, K to last st, M1, K1 (17 sts).

Purl 1 row.

Repeat last 2 rows three more times (23 sts).

Starting with a knit row, work 4 rows in SS.

Next row: K1, ssK, K to last 3 sts, K2tog, K1 (21 sts).

Purl 1 row.

Repeat last 2 rows three more times (15 sts).

Next row: K1, ssK, K6, turn work.

Next row: P3, turn work.

Working only over these 3 sts and starting with a knit row, work 4 rows in SS.

Next row: K3, K3 from unworked sts, K2tog, K1 (13 sts).

Next row: P1, P2tog, P to last 3 sts, P2togtbl, P1 (11 sts).

Cast off.

Wings: make two

Using black yarn, cast on 11 sts.

Next row: K5, sl1, K5.

Purl 1 row.

Repeat the last 2 rows three more times.

Next row: K1, ssK, K2, sl1, K2, K2tog, K1 (9 sts).

Purl 1 row.

Next row: K1, ssK, K1, sl1, K1, K2tog, K1 (7 sts).

Purl 1 row.

Next row: K1, ssK, sl1, K2tog, K1 (5 sts).

Purl 1 row.

Next row: Ssk, sl1, K2tog (3 sts).

Thread yarn through rem sts and fasten, leaving a length of yarn long enough to sew the wing up.

Feet: make two

Using yellow yarn, cast on 3 sts and, starting with a knit row, work 2 rows in SS.

Next row: (K1, M1) twice, K1 (5 sts).

Starting with a purl row, work 2 rows in SS.

Next row (WS): Knit (this forms a fold line).

Starting with a knit row, work 2 rows in SS.

Next row: K2tog, K1, ssK (3 sts).

Purl 1 row.

Thread yarn through rem sts and fasten, leaving a length of yarn long enough to sew the foot up.

Beak

Using yellow yarn, cast on 7 sts and, starting with a knit row, work 2 rows in SS.

Next row: K2tog, K1, (K2tog) twice (4 sts).

Thread yarn through rem sts and fasten. Sew side seam of beak.

Making up

Sew the body seam. This seam will be at the back of the penguin. Fill with toy stuffing. Fold the base of the penguin up and sew in place. Place the two beads on the head for eyes (bearing in mind the outer body will cover the top part of the head). Sew in place. It is easier to sew the eyes on before fitting the outer body onto the penguin. Pin the beak onto the face, using the photograph for guidance, and sew in place.

Sew the small seam on the outer body, this is the top. Place the outer body over the main body, placing the centre of the outer body at the centre back of the main body so that the tail is in the middle of the back.

Pin in place, stretching the edges slightly to get the right shape. Use the photograph for guidance. Sew in place and sew the small seam either side of the tail.

Fold each wing in half with WS together and sew the side seam. Pin the wings in place with the curved edge towards the front. It is a good idea to knit the sweater first and make sure the wings are in the right place for the 'wing holes' before sewing in place. Fold one of the feet in half along the purled fold line. Sew the side seams and repeat for the second foot. Pin into place on the base of the penguin, ensuring that the penguin will stand. Sew into place.

Sweater

Starting from the top.
Using red yarn, cast on 40 sts and work 8 rows in K2, P2 rib.
Change to green yarn.
Next row: K6, cast off 8 sts, K11, cast off 8 sts, K5 (leaving 6 sts, 12 sts and 6 sts).
Next row: P6, turn work and cast on 8 sts, turn work, P12, turn work and cast on 8 sts, turn work, P6 (40 sts).
*Change to red yarn.
Work 2 rows in SS.
Change to green yarn and, starting with a knit row, work 2 rows in SS.*
Work from * to * once more.
Change to red yarn and knit 1 row.
Work 4 rows in K2, P2 rib. Cast off in K2, P2 rib loosely and evenly.

Making up

Sew the seam of the sweater matching the stripes. The seam will be at the back of the sweater. Place on the penguin.

Gingerbread Folk

Materials

- 4-ply (fingering) yarn in brown, cream and red
- 5 x 8mm (⁵/₁₆in) decorative buttons
- 4 x 4mm (³/₁₆in) black beads
- Stitch holder or spare knitting needle
- Brown and red sewing cotton and sewing needle
- Toy stuffing

Needles

2.75mm (UK 12, US 2)

Size

9.5cm (3¾in) high

Instructions

Boy: make two

Left leg

Start with the left leg. Using brown yarn, cast on 5 sts and purl 1 row.

Next row: K1, M1, K3, M1, K1 (7 sts).

Purl 1 row.

Next row: K1, M1, K3, K2tog, K1 (7 sts).

Purl 1 row.

Repeat last 2 rows twice more.

Place sts on a stitch holder or spare knitting needle.

Right leg, body, arms and head

Using brown yarn, cast on 5 sts and purl 1 row.

Next row: K1, M1, K3, M1, K1 (7 sts).

Purl 1 row.

Next row: K1, ssK, K3, M1, K1 (7 sts).

Purl 1 row.

Repeat last 2 rows twice more.**

With RS facing, knit across 7 right leg sts and 7 left leg sts (14 sts).

Starting with a purl row, work 7 rows in SS.

*Continuing in SS, cast on 4 sts at beg of next 2 rows (22 sts).

Next row: K1, M1, K to last st, M1, K1 (24 sts).

Purl 1 row.

Next row: K1, ssK, K to end of row (23 sts).

Next row: P1, P2tog, P to end of row (22 sts).

Continuing in SS, cast off 8 sts at the beginning of the next 2 rows (6 sts).

Starting with a knit row, work 2 rows in SS.

Next row: K1, M1, K4, M1, K1 (8 sts).

Next row: P1, M1, P6, M1, P1 (10 sts).

Next row: K1, M1, K8, M1, K1 (12 sts).

Starting with a purl row, work 5 rows in SS.

Next row: K1, ssK, K6, K2tog, K1 (10 sts).

Purl 1 row.

Next row: K1, ssK, K4, K2tog, K1 (8 sts).

Next row: P1, P2tog, P2, P2togtbl, P1 (6 sts).

Cast off.*

Making up

Taking one piece of the gingerbread boy, sew the bead eyes in place using brown sewing cotton and a sewing needle. Sew the three buttons in place using matching sewing cotton. Place the two pieces of the gingerbread boy with WS together, then sew carefully around the edge using mattress stitch and placing a small amount of toy stuffing inside the body, head and limbs as you go.

Using red yarn and straight stitches, embroider his mouth. Using cream yarn and chain stitch, embroider the lines on the arms and legs. Using cream yarn and straight stitches, embroider his bow tie and hair. Use the photograph for guidance. For decorative stitches, see page 18.

Girl: make two

Legs

Make the legs, following the instructions for the gingerbread boy to **.

With RS facing, cast on 4 sts, knit across 7 right leg sts and 7 left leg sts, cast on 4 sts (22 sts).

Purl 1 row.

Next row: K1, ssK, K to last 3 sts, K2tog, K1 (20 sts).

Purl 1 row.

Repeat last 2 rows three more times (14 sts).

Follow instructions for gingerbread boy from * to *.

Making up

Sew the eyes in place and join the two pieces of the girl together following the instructions for the boy. Using cream yarn and blanket stitch (see page 12), embroider around the dress, right up to the shoulders, and create a neckline. Sew

the buttons in place on each shoulder using matching sewing cotton. Using red yarn and straight stitches, embroider her mouth. Using cream yarn and straight stitches, embroider her hair and finish off with a few stitches of red yarn on her hair. Use the photograph for guidance.

Candy Canes

Instructions

Note: The candy canes are made using the i-cord technique (see page 20), to avoid having a seam to sew up and give a really neat result. If you would perfer to knit them flat, work as follows:

Using sparkly white yarn, cast on 6 sts. Starting with a knit row and working in SS, work the following 5-row stripe pattern five times:

Work 3 rows in sparkly white yarn.

Work 2 rows in red yarn.

Thread yarn through rem st and fasten, leaving a length of yarn for sewing.

Candy canes: make three

Using sparkly white yarn, cast on 5 sts and work 2 rows in SS using the i-cord technique (see page 20).

Now follow this 5-row pattern to create the stripes:

Row 1: Knit 1 st using white yarn, K4 sts using red yarn.

Row 2: Knit 5 sts using red yarn.

Row 3: Knit 1 st using red yarn, knit 4 sts using white yarn.

Row 4: Knit 5 sts using white yarn.

Row 5: Knit 5 sts using white yarn.

Repeat this 5-row pattern four more times.

Repeat rows 1 and 2 once more.

Thread yarn through sts, do not gather or fasten rem yarn.

Holly leaves: make two

Using green yarn, cast on 2 sts and purl 1 row.

Next row: Kfb, YO, Kfb (5 sts).

Purl 1 row.

Next row: Cast off 1 st, K to end of row (4 sts).

Next row: Cast off 1 st, P to end of row (3 sts).

Next row: Kfb, K1, Kfb (5 sts).

Purl 1 row.

Next row: Cast off 2 sts, K to end of row (3 sts).

Next row: Cast off 2 sts, P to end of row (1 st).

Thread yarn through rem st and fasten.

Making up

If you have knitted your candy cane flat, place a chenille stick onto the WS of the work and, using the yarn from the gathered cast-off end, carefully sew the side seam to enclose the chenille stick. Gather the cast-on stitches and fasten. If you have used the i-cord technique, slide a chenille stick into the candy cane from the cast-on end. Once it is inside, gather the cast-on stitches and fasten. Gather and secure the cast-off end.

Sew the other two candy canes together in the same way.

Tie the canes together using gold ribbon, making a loop of ribbon to slide between the candy canes to hang them. Sew the holly leaves in place, using the photograph for guidance, and sew the beads in place with green yarn.

Materials

4-ply (fingering) yarn in sparkly white, red and green

3 x small red beads

Gold ribbon

3 x chenille sticks

Needles

2.75mm (UK 12, US 2)

Size

6.5cm (2½in) high with cane top bent over

Turkey

Instructions

Note: If you do not have sportweight yarn you could use DK instead. For the wrap and turn (w&t) technique, see page 12.

Body, head and tail

Using brown yarn and 3.5mm (UK 9/10, US 4) knitting needles, cast on 34 sts and, starting with a knit row, work 14 rows in SS. To shape the tail, work as follows:

Next row: K2, w&t.
Next row: P2.
Knit 1 row (all 34 sts).
Next row: P2, w&t.
Next row: K2.
Purl 1 row (all 34 sts).
Next row: Cast off 10 sts, K13, cast off 10 sts (leaving 14 sts in the centre of the work).
With WS facing, rejoin yarn to rem 14 sts and purl 1 row.
Next row: K1, ssK, K3, M1, K2, M1, K3, K2togtbl, K1 (14 sts).
Purl 1 row.
Repeat last 2 rows once more.
Starting with a knit row, work 4 rows in SS.
Next row: K1, ssK, K1, K2tog, K2, ssK, K1, K2tog, K1 (10 sts).
Next row: (P2tog, P1, P2togtbl) twice (6 sts).
Cast off.

Base

Using brown DK (8-ply) yarn and 3.5mm (UK 9/10, US 4) knitting needles, cast on 4 sts and purl 1 row.
Next row: K1, M1, K2, M1, K1 (6 sts).
Next row: P1, M1, P4, M1, P1 (8 sts).
Starting with a knit row, work 10 rows in SS.
Next row: K1, ssK, K2, K2tog, K1 (6 sts).
Next row: P1, P2tog, P2togtbl, P1 (4 sts).
Cast off.

Wings: make two

Using brown yarn and 3.5mm (UK 9/10, US 4) knitting needles, cast on 5 sts and knit 1 row.
Next row: P1, M1, P3, M1, P1 (7 sts).
Starting with a knit row, work 2 rows in SS.
Next row: K1, M1, K5, M1, K1 (9 sts).
Starting with a purl row, work 3 rows in SS.
Continuing in SS, cast off 1 st at beg of the next 2 rows (7 sts).
Continuing in SS, cast off 2 sts at beg of next 2 rows (3 sts).
Cast off.

Tail Feathers: make three

Dark brown section

Using dark brown yarn and 3mm (UK 11, US 2/3) knitting needles, cast on 7 sts and, starting with a knit row, work 2 rows in SS.
Next row: (K1, M1) six times, K1 (13 sts).
Purl 1 row.
Next row: (K2, M1) six times, K1 (19 sts).
Purl 1 row.
Next row: (K1, M1) twice, (K2, M1) six times, (K1, M1) three times, K2 (30 sts).
Purl 1 row.
Change to 3.5mm (UK 11, US 2/3) knitting needles.
Next row: (K2, P2) to last 2 sts, K2.
Next row: (P2, K2) to last 2 sts, P2.
Repeat last 2 rows twice more.
Next row: (K2, K2tog, YO) to last 2 sts, K2.
Next row: (P2, K2) to last 2 sts, P2.
Next row: (K2, P2) to last 2 sts, K2.
Repeat last 2 rows twice more.

Change to 3mm (UK 11, US 2/3) knitting needles.
Next row: (P2, K2tog) to last 2 sts, P2 (23 sts).
Next row: (K2, P1) to last 2 sts, K2.
Next row: (P2tog, K1) to last 2 sts, P2tog (15 sts).
Next row: (K2tog) six times, K1, K2tog (8 sts).
Next row: (P2tog) four times (4 sts).
Thread yarn through rem sts and fasten.

Orange section

Using orange yarn and 3mm (UK 11, US 2/3) knitting needles, cast on 7 sts and knit 1 row.
Next row: (P1, M1) six times, P1 (13 sts).
Starting with a knit row, work 2 rows in SS.
Next row: (K1, M1) four times, (K2, M1) twice, (K1, M1) three times, K2 (22 sts).
Purl 1 row.
Change to 3.5mm (UK 11, US 2/3) knitting needles.
Next row: (K2, P2) to last 2 sts, K2.
Next row: (P2, K2) to last 2 sts, P2.
Next row: (K2, P2) yo last 2 sts, K2.
Next row: (P2, K2tog, YO) to last 2 sts, P2.

Materials

DK (8-ply) yarn in brown

Sportweight (5-ply) yarn in dark brown, orange and a small amount of yellow

Small amount of red 4-ply (fingering) yarn

2 x 4mm (1/8in) black beads

Brown sewing cotton and sewing needle

Toy stuffing

Needles

3.5mm (UK 9/10, US 4) and 3mm (UK 11, US 2/3)

Size

9cm (3½in) high

Next row: (K2, P2) to last 2 sts, K2.
Next row: (P2, K2) to last 2 sts, P2.
Repeat last 2 rows once more.
Change to 3mm (UK 11, US 2/3) knitting needles.
Next row: (K2, P2tog) to last 2 sts, K2 (17 sts).
Next row: (P2tog, K1) to last 2 sts, P2tog (11 sts).
Next row: (K2tog) three times, K1, (K2tog) twice (6 sts).
Thread yarn through rem sts and fasten.

Brown section

Using brown yarn and 3.5mm (UK 9/10, US 4) knitting needles, cast on 4 sts and purl 1 row.
Next row: (K1, M1) three times, K1 (7 sts).
Purl 1 row.
Next row: (K1, M1) six times, K1 (13 sts).
Purl 1 row.
Next row: (K2tog, YO) six times, K1.
Purl 1 row.
Next row: (K2tog) six times, K1 (7 sts).
Purl 1 row.
Next row: (K2tog) three times, K1 (4 sts).
Cast off.

Beak

Using yellow yarn and 3mm (UK 11, US 2/3) knitting needles, cast on 6 sts and, starting with a knit row, work 2 rows in SS.
Next row: (K2tog) three times (3 sts).
Thread yarn through rem sts and fasten.

Beak piece

Using red yarn and 3mm (UK 11, US 2/3) knitting needles, cast on 3 sts and, starting with a knit row, work 4 rows in SS.
Next row: K1, K2tog (2 sts).
Starting with a purl row, work 4 rows in SS.
Thread yarn through rem sts and fasten.

Wattle: make two

Using red yarn and 3mm (UK 11, US 2/3) knitting needles, cast on 3 sts and, starting with a knit row, work 4 rows in SS.
Next row: (K1, M1) twice, K1 (5 sts).
Starting with a purl row, work 4 rows in SS.
Thread yarn through rem sts and fasten.

Making up

With WS together sew the seam from the top of the head, along the back and down the back seam of the body. Fill with toy stuffing. Pin the base in place, making sure the body is stuffed firmly enough. Sew the base in place. To make the head sit further back on the body, use brown yarn to stitch the back of the neck to the body, using the photograph as guidance. This makes the neck 'arch' backwards slightly and gives a more realistic look.

Pin the wings on the body, as shown in the photograph. To ensure there is enough room for the tail feathers, do not sew in place until you have pinned the tail feathers in place.

With the cast-on edge facing towards the front of the body, fold the largest dark brown) tail feather section in half with WS together and place over the end of the tail, using the photographs as guidance. Fold the middle (orange) tail feather section in half with WS together and pin in place on the turkey, in front of the larger tail feather section. Repeat for the smallest (brown) tail feather section. When you are happy with the placement, sew in place. Sew the sides and cast-on edge of each wing to the body, placing a small amount of toy stuffing inside the wing to give definition. Sew a stitch through the end of the wing near to the feather shaping, to stop the stuffing coming out, but leaving the feathers loose.

Sew the side seam of the beak and pin in place on the head, using the photograph for guidance. Sew in place. Sew in the ends and attach each wattle under the beak and sew in place. Sew the red beak piece in place on the top of the beak and then catch it in place at the side of the beak so that it hangs down one side. Use the photograph for guidance.

Using brown sewing cotton and a sewing needle, sew the beads in place for eyes on either side of the head.

Christmas Crackers

Instructions

Christmas cracker

Using main colour yarn, cast on 20 sts and, starting with a knit row, work 6 rows in SS.

Next row: (K2tog, YO) nine times, K2 (20 sts).

Starting with a purl row, work 6 rows in SS.

Next row (WS): Knit.

Knit 1 row.

Next row: (P2tog) ten times (10 sts).

Starting with a knit row, work 2 rows in SS.

Next row: (Kfb) ten times (20 sts).

Purl 1 row.

Knit 3 rows (the second row forms a fold line).

Purl 1 row.

Join in contrast colour yarn. From now on, work all sts marked as MC using main colour yarn, and all sts marked CC using contrast colour yarn.

Next row: (K3MC, K1CC) five times.

Next row: P2CC, (P1MC, P3CC) four times, P1MC, P1CC.

Starting with a knit row, work 4 rows in SS using contrast colour yarn. Do not break off main colour yarn.

Next row: K1CC, (K1MC, K3CC) four times, K1MC, K2CC.

Next row: (P1CC, P3MC) five times. Break off contrast colour yarn.

You will now be working using main colour yarn only.

Starting with a knit row, work 3 rows in SS.

Next row (WS): Knit (this row forms a fold line).

Knit 1 row.

Next row: (P2tog) ten times (10 sts).

Starting with a knit row, work 2 rows in SS.

Next row: (Kfb) ten times (20 sts).

Purl 1 row.

Knit 2 rows (the second row forms a fold line).

Starting with a knit row, work 6 rows in SS.

Next row: (K2tog, YO) nine times, K2 (20 sts).

Starting with a purl row, work 6 rows in SS.

Cast off.

Make a second cracker using grey, white and metallic silver yarns.

Materials

4-ply (fingering) yarn in red (main colour), yellow (contrast colour) and metallic gold

Make a second cracker using a double strand of grey laceweight yarn (main colour), sparkly white (contrast colour) and metallic silver

Toy stuffing

Needles

2.75mm (UK 12, US 2)

Size

9cm (3½in) long

Making up

Fold one end of the cracker so that WS are together and the fold is along the picot edge row. Sew the folded edge to the inside of the cracker, near to the purl row on the RS, which will form the fold line. Repeat for the other end. Roll the cracker up lengthwise and sew along the side seam, matching the purl lines and the pattern. Place toy stuffing inside the centre of the cracker only.

Gather the cracker in between the purl lines at each end, using the photograph for guidance, and secure. Using metallic gold yarn and chain stitch, embroider a line around the centre of the contrast colour yarn. Embroider a small French knot at the end of each contrast colour yarn 'point' using metallic gold yarn.

Elf

Instructions

Note: For the wrap and turn (w&t) technique, see page 12.

Head

Using pale pink yarn, follow instructions for the Santa Claus pattern on page 46.

Ears: make two

Using pale pink yarn, cast on 2 sts.
Next row: Kfb, K1 (3 sts).
Next row: P1, Pfb, P1 (4 sts).
Knit 1 row.
Next row: P1, P2tog, P1 (3 sts).
Next row: sl1, K2tog, psso (1 st).
Fasten off rem st.

Body

Using green yarn, cast on 8 sts and purl 1 row.
Next row: K2, M1, K4, M1, K2 (10 sts).
Next row: P2, M1, P1, M1, P4, M1, P1, M1, P2 (14 sts).
Next row: K3, M1, K1, M1, K6, M1, K1, M1, K3 (18 sts).

Starting with a purl row, work 10 rows in SS.
Next row (WS): Knit (this forms a fold line).
Next row: (K2tog) nine times (9 sts).
Next row: Purl.
Thread yarn through rem sts and fasten.

Jacket

Using green yarn, cast on 20 sts and, starting with a knit row, work 6 rows in SS.
Next row: (K2tog, YO) to last 2 sts, K2.
Starting with a purl row, work 9 rows in SS.
Next row: K2, ssK, K1, ssK, K6, K2tog, K1, K2tog, K2 (16 sts).
Next row: P1, P2tog, P1, P2tog, P4, P2togtbl, P1, P2togtbl, P1 (12 sts).
Thread yarn through sts and fasten.

Sleeves: make two

Using green yarn, cast on 7 sts and, starting with a knit row, work 4 rows in SS.
Next row: K1, M1, K5, M1, K1 (9 sts).
Starting with a purl row, work 3 rows in SS.
Change to red yarn and knit 4 rows.
Cast off.

Materials

4-ply (fingering) yarn in red, green, pale pink and black

Hand-dyed 4-ply (fingering) yarn in dark brown

Toy stuffing

2 x 3.4mm (^{1}/8in) black beads

20cm (8in) of 4-ply (fingering) yarn in metallic gold

1 x 6mm (^{3}/16in) brass bell

Black sewing cotton and sewing needle

Needles

2.75mm (UK 12, US 2)

Size

11cm (4^1/3in) tall

Hands: make two

Using pale pink yarn, cast on 4 sts and, starting with a knit row, work 8 rows in SS.
Cast off.

Legs: make two

Using green yarn, cast on 8 sts and, starting with a knit row, work 2 rows in SS.
Join in red yarn and work 2 rows in SS.
Repeat last 4 rows twice more.
Change to green yarn and work 2 rows in SS.
Cast off.

Boots: make two

Using black yarn, cast on 3 sts and, starting with a knit row, work 2 rows in SS.
Continuing in SS, cast on 5 sts at beg of the next 2 rows (13 sts).
Starting with a knit row, work 2 rows in SS.
Next row: K1, K2tog, K2, K2tog, K3, K2tog, K1 (10 sts).
Cast off using the three-needle cast-off technique (see page 21).

Belt

Using black yarn, cast on 3 sts and, starting with a knit row, work in SS until the belt, when slightly stretched, is long enough to go around the middle of the body.
Cast off.

Hat

Using red yarn, cast on 20 sts and knit 3 rows.

Change to green yarn and, starting with a knit row, work 6 rows in SS.

Next row: K9, w&t.

Next row: P5, w&t.

Next row: Knit to end of row.

Next row: (P2, P2tog) five times (15 sts).

Next row: K6, w&t.

Next row: Purl to end of row.

Next row: K8, K2tog, K1, K2tog, K2 (13 sts).

Starting with a purl row, work 3 rows in SS.

Next row: K1, K2tog, K3, K2tog, K2, K2tog, K1 (10 sts).

Starting with a purl row, work 3 rows in SS.

Next row: K1, K2tog, K4, K2tog, K1 (8 sts).

Starting with a purl row, work 3 rows in SS.

Next row: K1, K2tog, K2, K2tog, K1 (6 sts).

Purl 1 row.

Thread yarn through rem sts, leaving a length of yarn long enough to sew side seam of hat.

To make the collar, using red yarn, cast on 8 sts and purl 1 row.

Next row: (K1, M1) to last st, K1 (15 sts).

Purl 1 row.

Next row: (K1, M1) to last st, K1 (29 sts).

Purl 1 row.

Cast off as follows:

Cast off 2 sts, (cast on 2 sts, cast off 4 sts) to end of row.

Fasten off rem st, leaving a length of yarn for sewing.

Making up

Starting at the gathered cast-off edge of the body, sew the side seam, filling with toy stuffing as you go. Gather the cast-on edge, tighten and secure.

Taking the jacket, fold up the cast-on edge so that the picot row forms the fold line and sew the cast-on edge to the WS, making sure the stitches do not show on the RS. Place the jacket over the body with the open edges at the back and sew in place, sewing the seam as you go.

Sew the black belt around the middle of the body, catching the cast-on and cast-off edges together at the back of the body. Using the photograph as guidance, embroider the buckle using metallic gold yarn and straight stitches.

Sew the head together following the instructions on page 16, working the eyes, mouth, hair and blusher as instructed. Sew the head to the body, ensuring the seams are towards the back.

Taking the collar, and with the WS facing outwards, sew the seam, placing it at the back, and sew to the top of the body, making sure that the 'points' lie flat.

Using red yarn, sew the band of the hat together, change to green yarn and sew the remainder of the seam. Sew the bell firmly to the top of the hat. Place the hat on the elf's head, using the photograph for guidance and, using red yarn, carefully sew it in place. Taking the ears, pin them in place on either side of the head with the cast-off edge at the top. When you are happy with their position, sew in place to the face.

Sew the sleeves and hands together and attach them to the body following the making up instructions for Santa Claus on page 48.

Taking one of the boots, sew the seam up towards the cast-on stitches, filling the boot with a small amount of toy stuffing as you go. Pull the stitching to make the cast-on end 'curl' over slightly. Repeat for the second boot. Taking one of the legs, sew the seam together and sew the boot to the bottom edge of the leg, making sure that the seam is towards the back. Repeat for the second leg. Sew each leg in place at the front of the bottom of the body, under the jacket.

Tree Baubles

Instructions

Tree baubles

Using main colour (MC) yarn, cast on 14 sts and purl 1 row. The first row is written out in full to enable you to see the pattern of the increases.

Next row: K1, Kfb, K1, Kfb, Kfb, K1, Kfb, Kfb, K1, Kfb, Kfb, K1, Kfb, K1 (22 sts).

Purl 1 row.

Next row: K1, (Kfb, K3, Kfb) to last st, K1 (30 sts).

Purl 1 row.

Next row: K1, (Kfb, K5, Kfb) to last st, K1 (38 sts).

Purl 1 row.

Join in contrast yarn and work sts marked as CC using contrast colour yarn and all the other sts using main colour yarn.

Next row: K1, (Kfb, K3, K1CC, K3, Kfb) to last st, K1 (46 sts).

Next row: P6, (P1CC, P10) three times, P1CC, P6.

Next row: K1, (K1fb, K1, K7CC, K1, Kfb) to last st, K1 (54 sts).

Next row: P5, (P5CC, P8) three times, P5CC, P5.

Next row: K5, (K5CC, K8) three times, K5CC, K5.

Next row: P6, (P3CC, P10) three times, P3CC, P6.

Work decrease rows as follows:

Next row: K1, (ssK, K3, K3CC, K3, K2tog) to last st, K1 (46 sts).

Next row: P6, (P1CC, P10) three times, P1CC, P6.

Break off contrast colour yarn.

Next row: K1, (ssK, K7, K2tog) to last st, K1 (38 sts).

Purl 1 row.

Next row: K1, (ssK, K5, K2tog) to last st, K1 (30 sts).

Purl 1 row.

Next row: K1, (ssK, K3, K2tog) to last st, K1 (22 sts).

Purl 1 row.

Next row: K1, (ssK, K1, K2tog) to last st, K1 (14 sts).

Purl 1 row.

Thread yarn through rem sts, leaving a length of yarn long enough to sew the seam.

Finial

Using metallic gold yarn, cast on 8 sts and, starting with a knit row, work 3 rows in SS.

Next row: (P2tog) four times (4 sts).

Thread yarn through rem sts, leaving a length of yarn long enough to sew the seam and sew the finial to the bauble.

Materials

- 4-ply (fingering) yarn in red (main colour), green (contrast colour) and metallic gold
- Make a second bauble using a double strand of grey (main colour) and green 2-ply (laceweight) yarn (contrast colour) and metallic silver
- Toy stuffing
- 1 x 4cm (1½in) styrofoam ball

Needles
2.75mm (UK 12, US 2)

Size
5cm (2in) high

Making up

Using metallic gold yarn, embroider a small French knot at the top of each tree, leaving a length of yarn long enough between each French knot to ensure it will stretch when you place the bauble on the styrofoam ball.

Starting at the gathered end of the bauble and using mattress stitch, sew a few stitches along the seam of the bauble. Place the knitting over the styrofoam ball and continue to sew the seam until you reach the cast-on edge.

Run your needle and yarn through the cast-on sts and gather neatly. Secure and sew the end in.

Take the finial and, working from the gathered end, sew the small seam along the side. Place a tiny amount of toy filling in the finial and sew securely to the top of the bauble. To make the loop at the top of the finial, thread the yarn through the finial, leaving a loop, and secure. Thread the needle and yarn through the loop that this makes, and pass it through the working yarn. Tighten so that it appears as if there is a small knot on the loop of yarn. Repeat until you have worked all along the length of yarn forming the loop. This reinforces the loop. Fasten off the yarn.

Paper Chains

Instructions

Paper chains

Using green yarn, cast on 20 sts and knit
5 rows.
Cast off loosely and evenly.
Make four more links in green and five
links in each of the other colours.

Making up

Once you have decided the order in
which to sew your links together, carefully
sew the two short edges of the first link
together. Loop the second link through the
first link and sew the short seam on that
link. Repeat until all your links have been
looped and sewn together.

Materials
4-ply (fingering) yarn in green,
purple, yellow, blue
and fuchsia

Needles
2.75mm (UK 12, US 2)

Size
Each chain measures
approximately 3cm (1¼in)
when sewn; 25 links make a
finished chain approximately
55cm (21⅝in) long

Polar Bears

Instructions

Note: For the wrap and turn (w&t) technique, see page 12.

Head and body

Using sparkly white yarn, cast on 7 sts and purl 1 row.
Next row: (K1, M1) twice, K3, (M1, K1) twice (11 sts).
Purl 1 row.
Next row: K4, M1, K3, M1, K4 (13 sts).
Purl 1 row.
Next row: K5, M1, K3, M1, K5 (15 sts).
Next row: P6, M1, P3, M1, P6 (17 sts).
Next row: K1, M1, K6, M1, K3, M1, K6, M1, K1 (21 sts).
Next row: P15, w&t.
Next row: K9, w&t.
Next row: Purl to end of row.
Continuing in SS, cast on 3 sts at the beginning of the next 2 rows (27 sts).
Next row: Cast on 4 sts, K14, ssK, K3, K2tog, K10 (29 sts).
Next row: Cast on 4 sts, P13, P2tog, P3, P2togtbl, P13 (31 sts).
Next row: K12, ssK, K3, K2tog, K12 (29 sts).
Starting with a purl row, work 13 rows in SS.
Next row: K1, (ssK, K3, K2tog) four times (21 sts).
Purl 1 row.
Next row: K1, (ssK, K1, K2tog) four times (13 sts).
Cast off.

Ears: make two

Using sparkly white yarn, cast on 3 sts.
Next row: (Kfb) three times (6 sts).
Starting with a purl row, work 3 rows in SS.
Next row: (K2tog) three times (3 sts).
Cast off.

Legs: make four

Using sparkly white yarn, cast on 3 sts and purl 1 row.
Next row: (K1, M1) twice, K1 (5 sts).
Next row: P1, M1, P3, M1, P1 (7 sts).
Next row: K1, M1, K5, M1, K1 (9 sts).
Purl 1 row.
Next row: K1, M1, K7, M1, K1 (11 sts).
Starting with a purl row, work 7 rows in SS.
Next row: (K2tog) five times, K1 (6 sts).
Purl 1 row.
Thread yarn through rem sts and fasten.

Tail

Using sparkly white yarn, cast on 3 sts and, starting with a knit row, work 8 rows in SS.
Cast off.

Scarf

Using self-patterning sock yarn, cast on 6 sts and knit 1 row.
Next row: sl1, K5.
Repeat this row until scarf measures 17cm (6½in).

Making up

Starting at the cast-on edge of the head, gather the sts and fasten. Sew the seam under the head, filling with toy stuffing as you go. Continue sewing the seam underneath and up the back of the bear, stuffing with toy filling. Gather the cast-off edge and secure. Fold one of the ears in half with RS on the outside and the cast-on and cast-off edges together. Sew the seam along the bottom, gathering so that it pulls in either side of the ear to make a more rounded shape. Repeat for the second ear and pin in place using the photograph for guidance. For the eyes, pin the beads in place at either side of the three centre stitches. When you are happy with the position, sew the eyes in place using white sewing cotton and sew the ears on. Embroider the nose using black yarn and straight stitches.

Starting at the gathered cast-off end of one of the legs, sew the seam up to the start of the top shaping of the leg. Fill with toy stuffing. Repeat for the other three legs. Pin each leg in place, with the shaped top edge on the outside and using the photograph for guidance. Sew each leg firmly in place.

With WS together, fold the tail in half so that the cast-on and cast-off edges are together. Sew each side seam. Sew the tail to the back of the bear using the photograph for guidance. Sew the yarn ends into the scarf and knot the scarf around the bear's neck.

Materials

4-ply (fingering) yarn in sparkly white and a small amount of black

Self-patterning 4-ply (fingering) sock yarn

Make a second polar bear using fluffy white, pink and a small amount of black yarn

Toy stuffing

4 x black seed beads

White sewing cotton and sewing needle

Needles

2.75mm (UK 12, US 2)

Size

6cm (2³⁄₈in) high and 8cm (3¹⁄₈in) from nose to tail

Reindeer Heads

Instructions

Note: For the wrap and turn (w&t) technique, see page 12.

Head

Using brown tweed yarn, cast on 6 sts.
Next row: K1, (Kfb) four times, K1 (10 sts).
Purl 1 row.
Next row: K1, M1, K to last st, M1, K1 (12 sts).
Purl 1 row.
Repeat last 2 rows once more (14 sts).
Starting with a knit row, work 2 rows in SS.
Next row: K5, M1, K4, M1, K5 (16 sts).
Next row: P6, M1, P4, M1, P6 (18 sts).
Next row: K1, M1, K6, M1, K4, M1, K6, M1, K1 (22 sts).
Purl 1 row.
Next row: K1, M1, K8, M1, K4, M1, K8, M1, K1 (26 sts).
Purl 1 row.
Next row: K1, ssK, K6, ssK, K4, K2tog, K6, K2tog, K1 (22 sts).
Next row: P1, P2tog, P4, P2tog, P4, P2togtbl, P4, P2togtbl, P1 (18 sts).
Next row: K1, M1, K4, ssK, K4, K2tog, K4, M1, K1 (18 sts).
Next row: P1, M1, P5, P2tog, P2, P2togtbl, P5, M1, P1 (18 sts).
Next row: K1, M1, K5, ssK, K2, K2tog, K5, M1, K1 (18 sts).
Next row: P1, M1, P to last st, M1, P1 (20 sts).
Next row: K1, M1, K to last st, M1, K1 (22 sts).
Next row: P7, w&t.
Next row: Knit to end of row.
Next row: P1, M1, P to last st, M1, P1 (24 sts).
Next row: K7, w&t.
Next row: Purl to end of row.

Next row: K1, M1, K to last st, M1, K1 (26 sts).
Purl 1 row.
Cast off.

Base

Using brown tweed yarn, cast on 4 sts and purl 1 row.
Next row: K1, M1, K2, M1, K1 (6 sts).
Purl 1 row.
Next row: K1, M1, K4, M1, K1 (8 sts).
Next row: P1, M1, P6, M1, P1 (10 sts).
Starting with a knit row, work 4 rows in SS.
Next row: K1, ssK, K4, K2tog, K1 (8 sts).
Next row: P1, P2tog, P2, P2togtbl, P1 (6 sts).
Next row: K1, ssK, K2tog, K1 (4 sts).
Purl 1 row.
Cast off.

Ears: make two

Using brown tweed yarn, cast on 3 sts and, starting with a knit row, work 2 rows in SS.
Next row: (K1, M1) twice, K1 (5 sts).
Purl 1 row.
Next row: ssK, K1, K2tog (3 sts).
Next row: sl1, K2tog, psso (1 st).
Fasten off rem st.

Nose

Using red yarn, cast on 3 sts and purl 1 row.
Next row: (K1, M1) twice, K1 (5 sts).
Purl 1 row.
Next row: ssK, K1, K2tog (3 sts).
Thread yarn through rem sts.

Antlers: make two

Using dark brown yarn, cast on 6 sts and, starting with a knit row, work 14 rows in SS.
Thread yarn through rem sts and fasten.

Materials

4-ply (fingering) yarn in brown tweed, dark brown and red

Make a second head using sparkly white and grey 4-ply (fingering) yarn

2 x 4mm (1/8in) black beads

Black sewing cotton and sewing needle

Toy stuffing

Small piece of cardboard

Needles

2.75mm (UK 12, US 2)

Size

6.5cm (2½in) from base to top of head and 8cm (3⅛in) from nose to back edge

Antler pieces: make four

Using dark brown yarn, cast on 5 sts and, starting with a knit row, work 7 rows in SS.
Thread yarn through rem sts and fasten.

Making up

Starting at the cast-off edge, sew the seam which will be underneath the neck of the reindeer, gathering the cast-on edge to form the nose. Fill the head firmly with toy stuffing.

Using the base piece as a template, cut a piece of cardboard to fit just inside the base. Place the cardboard inside the reindeer and pin the base in place over the top of the cardboard. Sew in place. Taking the nose, run a gathering thread around the outside edge of the nose and pull up to make a bobble. Before securing, place a small amount of toy stuffing inside. Sew in place, using the photograph as guidance.

Taking one antler piece, sew the side seam, taking in one stitch on each edge to make the antler stronger. Repeat for the rest of the antler pieces. Sew one short piece to the long section on one side and the second piece on the other side, using the photograph for guidance. Repeat for the second antler.

Pin each ear in place, with the WS facing forward, on either side of the head and pin the antlers in between the ears. When you are happy with their position, sew firmly in place.

Using black sewing cotton, sew the beads in place for the eyes. Using a length of matching yarn, sew a loop at the back edge of the reindeer for hanging.

Christmas Lanterns

Instructions

Lanterns

Using black yarn, cast on 9 sts and purl 2 rows.

*Change to contrast colour yarn of your choice and, starting with a knit row, work 3 rows in SS, carrying the black yarn across the third row.

Change to black yarn and purl 1 row, carrying contrast colour behind work.

Change to contrast colour yarn and, starting with a knit row, work 3 rows in SS, carrying black yarn across third row.

Change to black yarn and purl 3 rows, carrying contrast colour yarn behind work on the third row.*

Repeat from * to * twice more.

Change to contrast colour yarn and, starting with a knit row, work 3 rows in SS, carrying black yarn across third row.

Change to black yarn and purl 1 row, carrying contrast colour yarn behind work.

Change to contrast colour yarn and, starting with a knit row, work 3 rows in SS. Cast off using contrast colour yarn.

Base

Using black yarn, cast on 7 sts and knit 9 rows.
Cast off.

Top of lantern

Using black yarn, cast on 41 sts and purl 2 rows.

Next row: P1, (ssK, K5, K2tog, P1) four times (33 sts).

Next row: K1, (P7, K1) four times.

Next row: P1, (ssK, K3, K2tog, P1) four times (25 sts).

Next row: K1, (P5, K1) four times.

Next row: P1, (ssK, K1, K2tog, P1) four times (17 sts).

Next row: K1, (P3, K1) four times.

Next row: P1, (sl1, K2tog, psso, P1) four times (9 sts).

Next row: P1, (P2tog) four times (5 sts).

Next row: K2tog, K3 (4 sts).

Work an i-cord (or in SS if you prefer) for the following 12 rows.

Thread yarn through rem sts and fasten.

Materials

4-ply (fingering) yarn in black (main colour) and small amounts in yellow, green, blue, pink and purple (contrast colours)

Toy stuffing

Needles
2.75mm (UK 12, US 2)

Size
6cm ($2^3/_5$in) high including loop

Making up

Taking the base and main part of the lantern, carefully sew the lower long edge to the base, matching the corners of the base to the purl row on each corner of the lantern. Sew the side seam to join the cast-on and cast-off edges. Fill with toy stuffing.

Sew the side seam of the top of the lantern. Using the photograph for guidance, loop over the i-cord and secure to make a loop at the top of the lantern (if you have knitted this section in SS you will need to sew the seam together first).

Pin the top of the lantern in place, matching the corners and with the top overhanging the lantern by 2 rows. Sew the top of the lantern in place and, if necessary, fill with more toy stuffing as you go, to give the top definition.

Using black yarn and chain stitch, embroider a line of stitches around the middle of the lantern to form the 'panes'. See photograph for guidance.

Holly Fairy

Instructions

Head

Using pale pink yarn, follow the instructions for Santa Claus on page 46.

Body

Using pale pink yarn, cast on 8 sts and purl 1 row.

Next row: K2, M1, K4, M1, K2 (10 sts).

Next row: P2, M1, P1, M1, P4, M1, P1, M1, P2 (14 sts).

Next row: K3, M1, K1, M1, K6, M1, K1, M1, K3 (18 sts).

Change to red yarn and, starting with a purl row, work 11 rows in SS.

Next row (RS): Purl (this forms a fold line).

Next row: (P2tog) nine times (9 sts).

Next row: Knit.

Thread yarn through rem sts and fasten.

Arms: make two

Using pale pink yarn, cast on 5 sts and, starting with a knit row, work 6 rows in SS.

Next row: K1, M1, K2, M1, K2 (7 sts).

Starting with a purl row, work 3 rows in SS.

Thread yarn through rem sts and fasten, leaving a long enough length of yarn to sew side seam.

Legs: make two

Using pale pink yarn, cast on 6 sts and, starting with a knit row, work 10 rows in SS.

Change to red yarn and, starting with a knit row, work 2 rows in SS.

Thread yarn through rem sts and fasten, leaving a length of yarn to sew the red part of the side seam.

Hair

Using dark brown hand-dyed yarn, cast on 7 sts and, starting with a knit row, work 2 rows in SS.

Continuing in SS, cast on 4 sts at the beginning of the next two rows (15 sts).

Continuing in SS, cast on 2 sts at the beginning of the next two rows (19 sts).

Starting with a knit row, work 8 rows in SS.

Next row: (K2, K2tog) four times, K3 (15 sts).

Starting with a purl row, work 3 rows in SS.

Next row: K1, K2tog, K2, K2tog, K1, K2tog, K2, K2tog, K1 (11 sts).

Purl 1 row.

Next row: K5, K2tog, K4 (10 sts).

Cast off rem 10 sts using the three-needle cast-off technique (see page 21).

Hair flick: make two

Using dark brown hand-dyed yarn, cast on 1 st.

Next row: Kfbf (3 sts).

Starting with a purl row, work 3 rows in SS.

Next row: (K1, M1) twice, K1 (5 sts).

Purl 1 row.

Next row: ssk, K3 (4 sts).

Next row: P2tog, P2 (3 sts).

Next row: sl1, K2tog, psso (1 st).

Thread yarn through rem st and fasten.

Skirt

Using red yarn, cast on 30 sts and purl 1 row.

Next row: (K4, M1) to last 2 sts, K2 (37 sts).

Starting with a purl row, work 7 rows in SS.

Next row: (K2tog) to last st, K1 (19 sts).

Knit 1 row.

Cast off.

Materials

4-ply (fingering) yarn in pale pink, red and dark green

2-ply (laceweight) yarn in fluffy mid-green

Hand-dyed 4-ply (fingering) yarn in dark brown

Toy stuffing

12 x 4mm (^{3}/$_{16}$in) red glass beads

2 x 3.4mm (^{1}/$_8$in) black beads

Black sewing cotton and sewing needle

Needles

2.75mm (UK 12, US 2)

Size

11cm (4¾in) high

Petticoat

Using fluffy mid-green yarn, cast on 54 sts and knit 4 rows.

Next row: (K1, K2tog) to end of row (36 sts).

Knit 1 row.

Cast off.

Holly leaves: make eight

Using dark green yarn, cast on 2 sts and purl 1 row.

Next row: Kfb, YO, Kfb (5 sts).

Purl 1 row.

Next row: Cast off 1 st, K to end of row (4 sts).

Next row: Cast off 1 st, P to end of row (3 sts).

Next row: Kfb, K1, Kfb (5 sts).

Purl 1 row.

Next row: Cast off 2 sts, K to the end of the row (3 sts).

Next row: Cast off 2 sts, P to end of row (1 st).

Thread yarn through rem st and fasten.

Making up

Starting at the gathered, cast-off edge of the body, sew the seam up towards the top, filling with toy stuffing as you go and changing yarn colour where the body colour changes. The seam will be at the back of the body. Using red yarn and chain stitch, embroider the 'shoulder straps' of the dress, using the photograph for guidance.

Sew the head together following the instructions on pages 16–17, adding eyes, mouth and blusher as instructed. Sew the head to the body.

Pin the hair to the head with the cast-off seam at the top centre of the head. Sew in place along the front edges, hiding the stitches in the knitting so that they do not show. Pin the two hair flicks in place either side of the central seam of the hair, using the photographs for guidance. Sew the cast-on and cast-off stitches securely to the head.

Sew two holly leaves to the back of the fairy's head, using the photograph as guidance, and then sew three beads in place using dark green yarn.

Pin the petticoat to the inside of the skirt, making sure that it just shows underneath the skirt. Sew in place making sure the stitches do not show on the right side of the skirt.

Pin the skirt to the body, using the photograph for guidance and placing the open edges at the back. Sew in place and sew the back seam of the skirt. Sew the holly leaf decorations in place using the photographs for guidance. Sew three beads in place where each pair of leaves meet using dark green yarn.

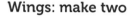

Wings: make two

Using fluffy mid-green yarn, cast on 4 sts and knit 1 row.
Next row: K1, M1, K to last st, M1, K1 (6 sts).
Rep last row once more (8 sts).
Knit 3 rows.
Next row: K1, K2tog, K2, K2tog, K1 (6 sts).
Knit 2 rows.
Next row: K2tog, K2, K2tog (4 sts).
Knit 6 rows.
Next row: K1, M1, K to last sts, M1, K1 (6 sts).
Knit 2 rows.
Next row: K1, M1, K to last st, M1, K1 (8 sts).
Knit 3 rows.
Next row: K1, K2tog, K2, K2tog, K1 (6 sts).
Knit 1 row.
Next row: K2tog, K2, K2tog (4 sts).
Knit 1 row.
Cast off.

Sew the seam on each leg using corresponding yarn colours and pin them in place at the front of the body. Sew in place. Pin the arms in place on either side of the body, making sure you are happy with their placement, and sew in place.

Take the wings and fold in half. Make a stitch at the top and bottom where the fold is and sew to the centre back of the body, positioning the lower edge just above the skirt.

Magic Elf Boots

Instructions

Note: For the wrap and turn (w&t) technique, see page 12.

Boots: make two

Using green yarn, cast on 4 sts.

Next row: K1, M1, K to last st, M1, K1 (6 sts).

Purl 1 row.

Repeat the last 2 rows once more (8 sts).

Next row: K6, w&t.

Next row: P4, w&t.

Next row: K4, w&t.

Next row: Purl to end of row.

Continuing in SS, cast on 12 sts at beg of next 2 rows (32 sts).

Starting with a knit row, work 8 rows in SS.

Next row: K13, ssK, K2, K2tog, K13 (30 sts).

Next row: P12, P2tog, P2, P2togtbl, P12 (28 sts).

Cast off.

Taking the knitted boot, with the RS facing you and the cast-on edge upwards, sew the seam using green yarn from the tip of the front of the boot (cast-on edge) along the sloped edge. The 'point' will curl over as you tighten the stitches. Lightly fill with toy stuffing to add definition. Continue to sew this seam along the top of the boot until 8 sts remain unsewn on either side. Fasten

off yarn. Unfold the boot so that the toe is towards you (with RS facing). Change to red yarn, pick up and knit 8 sts along the right-hand side of the boot, and a further 8 sts along the left-hand side (16 sts). You will now work the top edge and lining of the boot.

Starting with a purl row, work 2 rows in SS.

Knit 1 row (WS).

Purl 1 row.

Starting with a purl row, work 9 rows in SS. Cast off.

Boot cuff trims: make two

Using red yarn, cast on 17 sts and knit 1 row.

Cast off as follows:

Cast off 2 sts, (cast on 2 sts, cast off 4 sts) to end of row.

Fasten off rem st.

Making up

You will now have the boot with the lining attached to it. Taking the lining, which is above the boot at the moment, fold in half with RS together and sew the seam along the cast-off edge and side seam. The lining can now be pushed inside the boot so that the SS part forms the inside and the purl edge forms the top of the boot.

Using green yarn, sew the back seam of the boot. Lightly fill the rest of the boot with toy stuffing to add definition and shape to the boot, pushing a small amount of toy stuffing either side of the lining to make sure the shape of the boot is even along its length. Sew the seam along the bottom edge of the boot, gathering each end slightly to create rounded edges.

Sew the short side seams of the boot cuff trim together and place over the top of the boot with WS on the outside. Sew in place just under the purl edge, using the photograph for guidance. Using red sewing cotton and a sewing needle, sew a bead in

place at the end of each point of the trim. Sew a brass bell to the toe of each boot.

Taking a 50cm (19¾in) length of red yarn and a 50cm (19¾in) length of green yarn, knot them together at one end and twist them together until they twist back on themselves, making a twisted cord. Sew one end to the back of one boot in a loop, and the other end to the back of the other boot in a loop. Using the photograph for guidance, make a loop partway along the cord so the boots hang at different lengths.

Materials

4-ply (fingering) yarn in green and red

Toy stuffing

Red sewing cotton and sewing needle

16 x 3mm (¹/₈in) gold foil-lined beads

2 x 8mm (¼in) brass bells

Needles

2.75mm (UK 12, US 2)

Size

6cm (2³/₈in) long